AN INTRODUCTION
TO LAW AND ECONOMICS

AN INTRODUCTION
TO LAW AND ECONOMICS

A. MITCHELL POLINSKY

Professor of Law
Associate Professor of Economics
Stanford University

LITTLE, BROWN AND COMPANY
Boston and Toronto

Library of Congress Catalog Card No. 82-084438
ISBN 0-316-71277-9

Second Printing

ALP

Published simultaneously in Canada
by Little, Brown & Company (Canada) Limited

Printed in the United States of America

For

Guido Calabresi and Richard A. Musgrave

who introduced me
to law and economics

CONTENTS

CHAPTER 15

CHAPTER 16

LIST OF TABLES

PREFACE

This book grew out of a series of lectures given to a section of the first-year class at Stanford Law School in 1979-1980 and 1980-1981. Since I was allotted five weeks the first time and eight weeks the second, I could not possibly hope to comprehensively survey the many areas of law to which economic analysis has been applied. Moreover, this task had already been accomplished by others — most notably by Richard A. Posner in his well-known Economic Analysis of Law (2d ed. 1977). Instead, I chose to focus on a limited number of substantive issues and to emphasize "how to think like an economist" about them.

As economists know, thinking about a problem like an economist means building a "model" of it — either verbally, graphically, or mathematically — in order to distill the essence of the relationships being studied. Unfortunately for most law students and many undergraduates, much of the recent writing by economists about the legal system uses models that are graphical and/or mathematical. The goal of this book is to convey the spirit of the economic approach and the insights gained thereby without the technical apparatus. I will use nothing more complicated than simple numerical examples.

Because the book does not presume any knowledge of the legal system, it can be used both in law school and in undergraduate courses on law and economics. In either case, it can supplement a more comprehensive treatment of the subject, such as Posner's, or be used as the core text with additional material chosen by the instructor. Also, given the topics covered in the book, it can be used to supplement traditional casebooks in first-year law courses on property, contracts, torts, and criminal law, or casebooks in upper-level courses on environmental law.

In order to make the text flow as smoothly as possible, I have chosen to severely limit the number of footnotes. As a general rule, the only footnotes included are those that contain important qualifications or elaborations of points made in the text or that refer the reader to earlier or later discussions in the text. There are three minor exceptions to this rule. First, since I have tried to dispense with the technical terminology of economics as much as possible in the text, I have included some footnotes that relate ideas in the text to this terminology. Second, a few footnotes have been included that cite legal cases or doctrines relevant to points made in the text. And third, whenever the work of a specific author has been referred to in the text, the appropriate citation is included in a footnote. (However, the footnotes do not include any other references to the relevant scholarly literature on the economic analysis of law. Instead, a guide to the literature upon which the book is based is provided in a bibliographical appendix.)

I have received many helpful comments from colleagues and friends on earlier drafts of this book. For their efforts, I wish to thank Lucian Bebchuk, Jules Coleman, Robert Cooter, Robert Ellickson, Dorsey Ellis, Jr., Ronald Gilson, Henry Hansmann, Thomas Jackson, Mark Kelman, Alvin Klevorick, Lewis Kornhauser, Peter Menell, Richard Musgrave, Glen Nager, Jeffrey Perloff, Robert Rabin, William Rogerson, Roberta Romano, Daniel Rubinfeld, Steven Shavell, and Gregory Sidak. Their suggestions greatly improved the final product. I am also grateful to my wife, Joan Roberts Polinsky, for her valuable editorial suggestions, and to Barbara Adams for her help in preparing the manuscript for publication.

One final methodological note is in order before proceeding. Economic analysis has been used both to try to explain the legal system as it is and to recommend changes that might improve it. In the language of economists, these two approaches are referred to respectively as *positive* (or descriptive) economics and *normative* (or prescriptive) economics. As the reader will see, this book is normatively oriented. For each legal application considered, we will determine what legal rule or policy would best promote certain goals — with the primary focus on the goal of efficiency. Since the present legal system has undoubtedly been influenced by efficiency considerations, existing legal rules and policies will frequently correspond to those that are optimal in terms of efficiency. To this extent, the book will also provide an economic explanation of certain features of the present legal system.

AN INTRODUCTION
TO LAW AND ECONOMICS

CHAPTER 1
INTRODUCTION

When noneconomists want to make fun of economists (or when economists want to make fun of each other), they often tell the following story:

A shipwreck has left a physicist, a chemist, and an economist without food on a deserted island. A few days later a can of beans is washed up on the shore. The physicist proposes the following method of opening the can:

> I've calculated that the terminal velocity of a one-pound object — the weight of the can — thrown to a height of twenty feet is 183 feet per second. If we place a rock under the can the impact should just burst the seams without spilling the beans.

The chemist's response is:

> That's risky since we can't be sure we will throw it to the correct height. I've got a better idea. Let's start a fire and heat the can on the coals for one minute, thirty-seven seconds. I've calculated that this should just burst the seams. This method is less risky since we can always push the can off the fire if it starts to burst sooner.

The economist's reaction is:

> Both of your methods may work, but they are too complicated. My approach is much simpler: Assume a can opener.

If you have studied economics before, you will appreciate the significance of this joke (and probably already have heard it more than once). If you have not studied economics, you will soon learn why you should have laughed harder than you did. The can opener story contains one important truth and one important lie about economists. The truth is that they approach problems by making assumptions. The lie is that they make ridiculous assumptions (though, unfortunately, this is not always a lie).

The Role of Assumptions

Economists make assumptions for the obvious reason that the world, viewed economically, is too complicated to understand without some abstraction. To see this point in a legal context, consider for example the well-known products liability case of *Escola v. Coca Cola Bottling Co.*, in which the plaintiff was injured by an exploding bottle of soda. In a concurring opinion, Justice Traynor of the California Supreme Court made the following remarks:[1]

> I concur in the judgment [for the plaintiff], but I believe the manufacturer's negligence should no longer be singled out as the basis of a plaintiff's right to recover in cases like the present one. In my opinion it should now be recognized that a manufacturer incurs an absolute liability when an article that he has placed on the market, knowing that it is to be used without inspection, proves to have a defect that causes injury to human beings. . . . Even if there is no negligence, . . . public policy demands that responsibility be fixed wherever it will most effectively reduce the hazards to life and health inherent in defective products that reach the market. It is evident that the manufacturer can anticipate some hazards and guard against the recurrence of others, as the public cannot. Those who suffer injury from defective products are unprepared to meet its consequences. The cost of an injury and the loss of time or health may be an overwhelming misfortune to the person injured, and a needless one, for the risk of injury can be insured by the manufacturer and distributed among the public as a cost of doing business. It is to the public

1. Escola v. Coca Cola Bottling Co., 24 Cal. 2d 453, 461-462, 150 P.2d 436, 440-441 (1944).

interest to discourage the marketing of products having defects that are a menace to the public. If such products nevertheless find their way into the market it is to the public interest to place the responsibility for whatever injury they may cause upon the manufacturer, who, even if he is not negligent in the manufacture of the product, is responsible for its reaching the market. However intermittently such injuries may occur and however haphazardly they may strike, the risk of their occurrence is a constant risk and a general one. Against such a risk there should be general and constant protection and the manufacturer is best situated to afford such protection.

This excerpt from Justice Traynor's opinion implicitly raises several complicated questions but does not go very far in answering them. How is the criterion of "public policy" or "the public interest" to be defined? Should it take into account considerations of both efficiency and equity? What are the effects of the rules of negligence and absolute (or strict) liability on the care exercised by manufacturers in designing and producing products? On the care exercised by consumers in using products? On the price and output of the industry? Do the answers to these questions depend on whether the consumer misperceives the product risks? On whether the victim is a third party rather than a consumer of the product? Should the manufacturer be allowed to raise as a defense that the victim was contributorily negligent in the use of the product? Who is the better bearer of the product risks that are not eliminated — the manufacturer or the consumer? How does the answer to this question depend on whether the manufacturer can self-insure or purchase liability insurance? On whether the consumer can purchase first-party accident insurance or is covered by general social insurance programs? Unless you are already familiar with the economics literature on products liability, you probably cannot answer many of these questions in a systematic way. By the end of this book, however, you should be able to answer all of them by thinking about them like an economist.

The way an economist would go about answering these questions would be to isolate one or two of them at a time by making simplifying assumptions that eliminate the others. For example, one might start with the case in which the victim is a consumer of the product and assume that he has perfect information about the product risks, that he does not affect the probability or magnitude of the harm by his own actions, and that he is "risk neutral."[2] It is relatively straightforward in this framework to determine what effects the rules of negligence and strict liability will have on the care exercised by manufacturers and on the price and output of the industry. One could then investigate the consequences of adding the following complications to this framework: consumer misperceptions, joint determination by the manufacturer and the consumer of the probability and magnitude of harm, and "risk aversion" of the consumer (and, possibly, of the manufacturer).[3] The last complication — risk aversion — would have to be considered both when insurance was and was not assumed to be available.

Each of the special cases just described — corresponding to a particular set of assumptions — can be analyzed relatively easily because only a few issues are considered at a time. Even though each special case is admittedly unrealistic by itself, it will generate some insights that are relevant to real products liability problems. And by examining all of the cases, one will have obtained a comprehensive — and, more important, comprehensible — perspective on the economics of product liability rules.

This discussion of the role of simplifying assumptions in the economic analysis of product liability rules applies to every problem addressed by economists — including every topic considered in this book. The art of economics is picking assumptions that simplify a problem enough to better understand certain features of it, without inevitably causing those features to be unimportant ones. That economists are sometimes thought to eliminate what is interesting about a problem through their assumptions is what gives the can opener story its bite.

What has been said thus far is meant to be a warning, not an apology. Be prepared to accept (at least for a while) some obviously unrealistic assumptions. By the end of this book, I hope to convince you that there are many insights to be gained from the economic analysis of law and that these insights are the result of the artful choice of simplifying assumptions.

2. The term "risk neutral" is defined at p. 27 below.
3. The concept of risk aversion is explained at p. 51 below.

The plan of the book is somewhat unconventional. Chapters introducing basic economic concepts will be interwoven with chapters applying those concepts to legal problems. In this manner, the relevant economic ideas will receive systematic development for readers not trained in economics, and readers with some training in economics can easily identify and skip the material with which they are familiar. The economic concepts to be developed include efficiency and equity, risk bearing and insurance, and competitive markets. These concepts will be applied to nuisance law, breach of contract, automobile accidents, law enforcement, pollution control, and products liability. Also, in the concluding chapter, some problems with the practical implementation of the economic approach to law will be discussed.

The subject matter is introduced in stages of increasing complexity, both to simplify the exposition and to better convey the style of economic analysis. For example, breach of contract remedies are first examined in Chapter 5 in a contractual relationship in which the parties are assumed to be risk neutral. This chapter analyzes the effects of the remedies on the parties' breach decisions and on their "reliance" expenditures. Then, in Chapter 7, the concept of risk aversion is introduced (and the function of insurance is discussed). In Chapter 8, breach of contract remedies are reexamined under the more realistic assumption that the parties may be risk averse. That chapter focuses on the effects of the remedies on the allocation of risk from breaches that do occur. By developing the analysis in these stages, it is easier to see the separate economic functions of breach of contract remedies — to control the behavior of contracting parties with respect to breach and reliance decisions, and to allocate the risks of breaches that do occur. The same pattern is repeated for the discussion of automobile accidents, while the development of each of the other topics — nuisance law, pollution control, law enforcement, and products liability — is contained within a single chapter.

CHAPTER 2

EFFICIENCY AND EQUITY

For purposes of this book, the term *efficiency* will refer to the relationship between the aggregate benefits of a situation and the aggregate costs of the situation;[4] the term *equity* will refer to the distribution of income among individuals.[5] In other words, efficiency corresponds to "the size of the pie," while equity has to do with how it is sliced. Economists traditionally concentrate on how to maximize the size of the pie, leaving to others — such as legislators — the decision how to divide it. The attractiveness of efficiency as a goal is that, under some circumstances described below, everyone can be made better off if society is organized in an efficient manner.

Is There a Conflict?

One important question is whether there is a conflict between the pursuit of efficiency and the pursuit of equity. If the

4. This popular concept of efficiency is more intuitive than the technical concept of efficiency known as *Pareto efficiency* or *Pareto optimality* (after the Italian economist Vilfredo Pareto). A situation is said to be Pareto efficient or Pareto optimal if there is no change from that situation that can make someone better off without making someone else worse off. Equivalently, if a situation is *not* efficient in this sense, then, by definition, someone *can* be made better off without making anyone else worse off. Every conclusion in this book regarding the efficiency of a legal rule or policy can be derived in terms of Pareto efficiency or Pareto optimality. I have opted for the more intuitive concept of efficiency used in the text for expositional simplicity.

5. This is the standard sense in which economists use the term *equity*. However, lawyers and philosophers often use this term differently. For example, *equity* might refer to the process by which income or wealth is acquired (as opposed to its final distribution), or to the degree to which exogenously determined rights are protected.

pie can be sliced in any way desired, then clearly there is no conflict — with a bigger pie, everyone can get a bigger piece. If, however, in order to create a bigger pie, its division must be quite unequal, then, depending on what constitutes an equitable division of the pie, there may well be a conflict between efficiency and equity. It may be preferable to accept a smaller pie (less efficiency) in return for a fairer division (more equity).

The potential conflict between efficiency and equity can be illustrated by a simple example. Suppose that the government must decide whether to build a dam and that the Dean of Stanford Law School and I are the only two individuals affected by it. Currently, without the dam, the Dean has $65 and I have $35, so total income is $100. The dam would cost $30 to build, consisting of $30 worth of my labor but none of the Dean's. The dam would create benefits worth $40, all of which would go to the Dean because the only feasible location for building the dam happens to be on his property. Should the dam be built?

On efficiency grounds, the dam clearly should be built since it creates benefits of $40 and costs only $30, thereby creating net benefits of $10. But the equity effects need to be considered as well. Before the dam is built, the Dean had $65 and I had $35. After the dam is built, the Dean has $105 (including the $40 benefit) and I have $5 (after subtracting my $30 cost). Whether these distributional consequences are desirable depends on what constitutes a fair distribution of income. Suppose that the most equitable distribution of income involves the Dean receiving 60 percent of total income and my receiving 40 percent. If the dam is not built, then the Dean should have $60 and I should have $40. If the dam is built and total income rises by $10, the Dean should have $66 and I should have $44.

But suppose, regardless of whether the dam is built, it is impossible to redistribute income between the two of us. Therefore, the choice is between the Dean's having $65 and my having $35 if the dam is not built, and the Dean's having $105 and my having $5 if the dam is built. Building the dam is more efficient but less equitable. How this conflict between efficiency and equity should be resolved depends on how important efficiency is relative to equity. If promoting equity is very important, it might be desirable to sacrifice some efficiency for more equity by not building the dam (in other words, "damn" the Dean).

Alternatively, suppose it is possible to costlessly redistribute income between the Dean and me. Then, given the preferred distribution of income, if the dam is not built, $5 would be transferred from the Dean to me, so he would end up with $60 and I would have $40. If the dam is built, $39 would be transferred to me, so he would have $66 and I would have $44. Clearly, since total income is distributed according to the percentages desired and we both are better off with the dam, the dam should be built. There is no conflict between efficiency and equity.

Note that, if it is possible to redistribute income at no cost, the dam should be built regardless of what constitutes an equitable distribution of income. If, for example, an egalitarian income distribution is desired, then without the dam the Dean and I could each have $50 and with the dam we could each have $55. If, alternatively, equity required that everything should go to the Dean, the dam should be built because he could then have $110 rather than $100.

The dam example illustrates two important general observations. If income cannot be costlessly redistributed, there may be a conflict between efficiency and equity. Whether there is in fact a conflict depends on the specific distributional consequences of pursuing efficiency and on what constitutes an equitable distribution of income. However, if income can be costlessly redistributed, there is no conflict between efficiency and equity. This is true regardless of the specific distributional consequences of pursuing efficiency and regardless of what constitutes an equitable distribution of income. In other words, if income can be costlessly redistributed, it is always preferable to maximize the size of the pie since the pie can be sliced in any way desired.

Whether income can be costlessly redistributed is discussed in Chapter 14. Although the conclusion there is that income redistribution is in general costly, it is argued nonetheless that efficiency should be the principal criterion for evaluating the legal system. This argument rests on the observations, explained at length in Chapter 14, that it is often impossible to redistribute income through the choice of legal rules and that, even when it is possible, redistribution through the government's tax and transfer system may be cheaper and is likely to be more precise. In other words, the potential conflict between efficiency and equity when income is costly to redistribute should be considered in the design of the government's tax and transfer system, but not generally in the choice of legal rules. Thus, *for purposes of discussing the legal system,* a reasonable simplifying assumption is that income can be costlessly redistributed. This assumption will be maintained until Chapter 14 (although the distributional consequences of legal rules will occasionally be noted).

Before proceeding, it is worth mentioning several other standard assumptions of economic analysis that will be made in analyzing the efficiency of legal rules. First, all benefits and costs can be measured in terms of a common denominator — dollars. It is important to emphasize that this assumption is made for expositional simplicity. It is not essential to economic analysis and does not exclude considerations that might be thought of as noneconomic — such as the protection of life and limb.[6] Second, individuals themselves determine the dollar values to place on their benefits and costs. This is known as the assumption of *consumer sovereignty.* It is an acceptable assumption if one believes that individuals generally know what is best for themselves. Third, the values placed by individuals on their benefits and costs are "stable" in the sense that these values are not affected by changes in public policy. For example, an individual's evaluation of the desirability of cleaner air is assumed not to depend on whether the legal system establishes a right to clean air. This is known as the assumption of *exogenous preferences.* Finally, individuals (and, when relevant, firms) maximize their benefits less their costs. This is known as the assumption of *utility maximization* (or, when firms are involved, profit maximization).

6. However, to incorporate benefits and costs that are not equivalent to a gain or loss of money would require the introduction of economic concepts that are beyond the scope of this book.

CHAPTER 3

THE COASE THEOREM

One of the central ideas in the economic analysis of law was developed in an article by Ronald Coase in 1960.[7] This idea, which has since been named the *Coase Theorem*, is most easily described by an example. Consider a factory whose smoke causes damage to the laundry hung outdoors by five nearby residents. In the absence of any corrective action each resident would suffer $75 in damages, a total of $375. The smoke damage can be eliminated in either of two ways: A smokescreen can be installed on the factory's chimney, at a cost of $150, or each resident can be provided an electric dryer, at a cost of $50 per resident. The efficient solution is clearly to install the smokescreen since it eliminates total damages of $375 for an outlay of only $150, and it is cheaper than purchasing five dryers for $250.

Zero Transaction Costs

The question asked by Coase was whether the efficient outcome would result if the right to clean air is assigned to the residents or if the right to pollute is given to the factory. If there is a right to clean air, then the factory has three choices: pollute and pay $375 in damages, install a smokescreen for $150, or purchase five dryers for the residents at a total cost of $250. Clearly, the factory would install the smokescreen, the efficient solution. If there is a right to pollute, then the residents face three choices: suffer their collective damages of $375, purchase

7. Ronald H. Coase, The Problem of Social Cost, 3 J. L. & Econ. 1 (1960).

five dryers for $250, or buy a smokescreen for the factory for $150. The residents would also purchase the smokescreen. In other words, the efficient outcome would be achieved regardless of the assignment of the legal right.

It was implicitly assumed in this example that the residents could costlessly get together and negotiate with the factory. In Coase's language, this is referred to as the assumption of *zero transaction costs*. In general, transaction costs include the costs of identifying the parties with whom one has to bargain, the costs of getting together with them, the costs of the bargaining process itself, and the costs of enforcing any bargain reached. With this general definition in mind, we can now state the simple version of the Coase Theorem: If there are zero transaction costs, the efficient outcome will occur regardless of the choice of legal rule.

Note that, although the choice of the legal rule does not affect the attainment of the efficient solution when there are zero transaction costs, it does affect the distribution of income. If the residents have the right to clean air, the factory pays $150 for the smokescreen, whereas if the factory has the right to pollute, the residents pay for the smokescreen. Thus, the choice of the legal rule redistributes income by the amount of the least-cost solution to the conflict. Since it is assumed for now that income can be costlessly redistributed, this distributional effect is of no consequence — if it is not desired, it can be easily corrected.

Positive Transaction Costs

The assumption of zero transaction costs obviously is unrealistic in many conflict situations. At the very least, the disputing parties usually would have to spend time and/or money to get together to discuss the dispute. To see the consequences of positive transaction costs, suppose in the example that it costs each resident $60 to get together with the others (due, say, to transportation costs and the value attached to time). If the residents have a right to clean air, the factory again faces the choice of paying damages, buying a smokescreen, or buying five dryers. The factory would again purchase the smokescreen, the efficient solution. If the factory has a right to pollute, each resident now has to decide whether to bear the losses of $75, buy a dryer for $50, or get together with the other residents for $60 to collectively buy a smokescreen for $150. Clearly, each resident will choose to purchase a dryer, an inefficient outcome. Thus, given the transaction costs described, a right to clean air is efficient, but a right to pollute is not.

Note that in the example the preferred legal rule minimized the effects of transaction costs in the following sense. Under the right to clean air, the factory had to decide whether to pay damages, install a smokescreen, or buy five dryers. Since it was not necessary for the factory to get together with the residents to decide what to do, the transaction costs considered — the costs of the residents to get together — did not have any effect. Under the right to pollute, the residents had to decide what to do. Since the residents were induced to choose an inefficient solution in order to avoid the cost of getting together, the transaction costs did have an effect. Thus, even though no transaction costs were actually incurred under the right to pollute since the residents did not get together, the effects of transaction costs were greater under that rule.

We can now state the more complicated version of the Coase Theorem: If there are positive transaction costs, the efficient outcome may not occur under every legal rule. In these circumstances, the preferred legal rule is the rule that minimizes the effects of transaction costs. These effects include the actual incurring of transaction costs and the inefficient choices induced by a desire to avoid transaction costs.

The distributional consequences of legal rules are somewhat more complicated when there are transaction costs. It is no longer true, as it was when there were zero transaction costs, that the choice of rule redistributes income by the amount of the least-cost solution. In the example, if the residents have the right to clean air, the factory pays $150 for the smokescreen, whereas if the factory has the right to pollute, the residents pay $250 for five dryers.

Although the simple version of the Coase Theorem makes an unrealistic assumption about transaction costs, it provides a useful way to begin thinking about legal problems because it suggests the kinds of transactions that would have to occur under each legal rule in order for that rule to be efficient. Once these required transactions are identified, it may be apparent that, given more realistic assumptions about transaction costs, one rule is clearly preferable to another on efficiency grounds. The more complicated version of the Coase Theorem provides a guide to choosing legal rules in this situation. All of the applications investigated in this book — nuisance law, breach of contract, automobile accidents, law enforcement, pollution control, and products liability — can be approached in this way, although some fit more naturally into the Coasian framework than others.

CHAPTER 4

FIRST APPLICATION — NUISANCE LAW

One area of law that can be readily examined in terms of the Coase Theorem is nuisance law. Nuisance cases result from incompatible land uses and typically involve a small number of individuals bargaining with each other, as when emissions from a factory fall upon neighboring property, bright lights or noise disturb someone's sleep, or an unsightly building mars an attractive residential neighborhood.

Adopting a framework first suggested by Guido Calabresi and Douglas Melamed,[8] the resolution of a nuisance dispute may be viewed as involving two steps. First, an *entitlement* must be chosen — that is, a determination must be made as to who is entitled to prevail. The injurer can be granted the right to engage in the activity that causes harm, or the victim can be granted the right to be free from harm. Then, a decision must be made how to protect the entitlement. One possibility is to grant the holder of the entitlement an *injunction.* If the victim holds the entitlement, protecting it by an injunction means that he can prohibit the injurer from causing harm. Thus, the injurer can cause damage only if he "buys off" the victim. Similarly, if the injurer holds the entitlement, protecting it by an injunction means that the victim must buy off the injurer if he wants damages reduced.

An alternative method of protecting entitlements is to give the holder of the entitlement an amount of money — *damages*

8. Guido Calabresi & A. Douglas Melamed, Property Rules, Liability Rules and Inalienability: One View of the Cathedral, 85 Harv. L. Rev. 1089 (1972).

TABLE 1

Nuisance Law Example

Output of Factory	Additional Profits of Factory	Total Profits of Factory	Additional Damages of Resident	Total Damages of Resident	Total Profits Less Total Damages
0	—	$0	—	$0	$0
1	$10,000	$10,000	$1,000	$1,000	$9,000
2	$4,000	$14,000	$15,000	$16,000	−$2,000
3	$2,000	$16,000	$20,000	$36,000	−$20,000

— that some governmental body such as a court determines. If the victim has the entitlement, he has the right to be compensated, but he cannot prohibit the injurer from causing harm as he could under an injunctive remedy.[9] Analogously, if the injurer holds the entitlement, protecting it by a damage remedy would mean that the victim could restrict the injurer's activity but would have to compensate the injurer for the injurer's "damages" (for example, forgone profits). This last combination — entitling the injurer to damages — is very unconventional, but it has been used.[10] Thus, there are four possible solutions, corresponding to who is given the entitlement and how it is protected.

In this chapter, we will examine whether the efficiency criterion can determine which entitlement to choose and which remedy to use to protect it. The analysis will be undertaken through an example of a polluting factory next to a single resident. The factory can produce zero, one, two, or three units of output. At each level of output, the factory earns a certain level of profits, and the resident suffers some level of damages. The facts of the example are described in Table 1. Maximizing the

9. The leading American nuisance case illustrating this version of the damage remedy is Boomer v. Atlantic Cement Co., 26 N.Y.2d 219, 257 N.E.2d 870, 309 N.Y.S.2d 312 (1970).

10. See Spur Industries, Inc. v. Del E. Webb Development Co., 108 Ariz. 178, 494 P.2d 700 (1972).

size of the pie is equivalent to maximizing the factory's profits net of the resident's damages. Given the data in Table 1, this occurs when the factory produces one unit of output. Thus, one unit of output is the efficient solution in the example.

Zero Transaction Costs

We know from the discussion in the previous chapter that if there are zero transaction costs, then the factory will end up producing the efficient output regardless of the choice of remedy or entitlement. It will be useful to see how this comes about in the example before considering more realistic assumptions about transaction costs.

Under the injunctive remedy, suppose, for example, that an entitlement to clean air is given to the resident. This corresponds to giving the resident the right to force the factory to produce zero output. The factory, however, would gain $10,000 in profits from producing one unit, and the resident would suffer only $1,000 in damages. Thus, it is in both parties' interest to reach an agreement under which the factory would pay the resident some amount between $1,000 and $10,000 for permission to produce one unit. Assuming zero transaction costs, which is interpreted to imply cooperative behavior, such an agreement will be reached. It will not be mutually beneficial for the factory to produce a second unit since the factory would gain only an additional $4,000, whereas the resident would suffer an additional $15,000 in damages. Similarly, it would not be mutually beneficial for the factory to produce three units. Thus, the parties would remain at one unit, the efficient solution.

Under the damage remedy, suppose that an entitlement to clean air is given to the resident, as before, and that the court makes the factory liable for the resident's actual damages. Since the factory would gain $10,000 from producing one unit and would be liable for only $1,000, the factory clearly will choose to produce at least one unit. It will not be in the factory's interest to produce the second unit since the increase in the factory's profits is $4,000 and its additional liability is $15,000. Similarly, the factory would be worse off if it produced three units. Thus, the factory would choose to produce the efficient output.

Strategic Behavior

The assumption of zero transaction costs is obviously unrealistic in many respects. We will first consider the possibility that the parties may behave strategically;[11] in other words, to establish reputations as tough bargainers, they may adopt "hold-out" tactics. If both parties are stubborn, they may not be able to reach an agreement even when both could be made better off. Such behavior is not uncommon; for example, parties often go to court rather than settle out of court more cheaply.[12] We will now reconsider the nuisance remedies assuming that the parties behave strategically.

Under the injunctive remedy with an entitlement to clean air, we saw that it would be in both parties' interest to reach an agreement in which the factory paid the resident some amount between $1,000 and $10,000. However, because of strategic behavior, the resident may, for example, hold out for $8,000, while the factory may refuse to pay anything over $5,000. As a result, the resident might enforce the injunction and shut down the factory (at least for some period), an inefficient outcome.

The problem of strategic behavior under the injunctive remedy can be overcome by the appropriate choice of the entitlement. Instead of an entitlement corresponding to zero output of the factory — an *absolute* entitlement to clean air — suppose the court were to choose an entitlement corresponding to one unit of output — an *intermediate* entitlement. Under the injunctive remedy, this would mean that the factory could produce one unit, but no more, without having to obtain the permission of the resident. Starting at one unit of output, it would not be mutually beneficial to produce a second or third unit since the factory's gains are less than the resident's losses. Likewise, it would not be mutually beneficial to reduce output to zero since the resident's gain (in the form of reduced damages)

11. Although strategic behavior does not necessarily generate any out-of-pocket costs or costs associated with lost time, it will be treated as a type of transaction cost. It is like other transaction costs in that it may prevent the parties from reaching an efficient agreement.

12. There may be reasons other than strategic behavior why parties litigate rather than settle. For example, the parties may disagree about the plaintiff's chance of winning at trial and therefore not perceive a mutually beneficial settlement.

is less than the factory's losses (in the form of reduced profits). Thus, starting at an intermediate entitlement of one unit, the parties will remain there. In essence, the reason strategic behavior cannot upset this outcome is that there are no beneficial changes that can be made and that would require negotiation.

This discussion illustrates a general principle: Under the injunctive remedy, in order to overcome strategic behavior it is necessary to choose an entitlement corresponding to the efficient outcome. This is because, starting from any other entitlement, the parties must reach some kind of an agreement to get to the efficient outcome; strategic behavior may prevent this agreement from being reached.

Under the damage remedy with an entitlement to clean air and liability equal to actual damages, we saw that the factory would choose to produce the efficient output of one unit. The presence of strategic behavior does not affect this result because there are no bargains that the parties have to reach. Also, there are no threats the factory can make because, given that the factory is liable for actual damages, the resident is indifferent among all levels of the factory's output.

That liability equals actual damages is crucial to the conclusion of the previous paragraph. To see why, suppose the factory's liability is $7,000 for the first unit — exceeding the resident's damages of $1,000 — and, as before, equal to the resident's damages for the second and third units. If the factory produces one unit of output it will gain $3,000 ($10,000 − $7,000). The resident will also gain $6,000, the amount by which the liability payment exceeds actual damages ($7,000 − $1,000). But the factory can deny this gain to the resident by not producing the first unit of output. Therefore, if the factory believes that it can bargain more effectively than the resident, it may threaten to not produce unless the resident pays some specified amount up to his full gain of $6,000. However, if the resident believes that he is the better bargainer, he may not give in to the factory's demand. As a result, the factory may carry out its threat, if only to make future threats credible, and produce at an inefficient output.

The kind of stubborn bargaining or "extortion" just described cannot occur if liability is equal to actual damages. Since the resident is not overcompensated, and so gains nothing from an increase in the factory's output, the factory's threat to not produce the first unit of output has no effect. With full compensation, the resident is indifferent as to whether the first unit is produced and is likewise indifferent with respect to the second and third units. Thus, the factory will maximize its after-liability profits by increasing production to the efficient output of one unit.

This discussion illustrates another general principle: Under the damage remedy, to overcome strategic behavior it is necessary to set liability equal to actual damages. If liability exceeds actual damages, then the party who is liable has an incentive to threaten to deny the other party's overcompensation by choosing an inefficient outcome.[13]

Imperfect Information

The analysis of strategic behavior under the injunctive and damage remedies suggests another way in which the assumption of zero transaction costs is likely to be unrealistic. For both remedies, it was seen that it is necessary for the court to have certain information about the nuisance dispute in order to achieve the efficient solution. Under the injunctive remedy, the court needs to know the efficient outcome in order to choose an entitlement corresponding to it. And under the damage remedy, the court needs to know the resident's damages in order to set liability equal to actual damages. It was implicitly assumed that the court had whatever information was required. We will now reconsider the remedies when this information is incomplete. The assumption of strategic behavior will be maintained in this discussion.

Suppose the court has limited information of the following sort: It knows the resident's schedule of damages but does not

13. More generally, strategic behavior can be overcome under the damage remedy if liability is less than or equal to actual damages up to the efficient output and greater than or equal to actual damages beyond the efficient output. It is beyond the scope of this chapter to explain this more general proposition. Note, however, that the statements and examples in the text are consistent with it.

know the factory's schedule of profits. For example, the court might be able to easily obtain information about the damage to property from pollution but not about the cost to the polluter of changing production methods to abate pollution.[14]

Under the injunctive remedy, the court no longer can achieve the efficient outcome. To reach that outcome, strategic behavior must be avoided, which requires under the injunctive remedy that the entitlement coincide with the efficient output. But to determine the efficient output, the court must know when the factory's profits net of the resident's damages are maximized. Knowledge of the damage schedule alone obviously is insufficient to determine this level of output. Although the court could guess the efficient output, if it makes a mistake, as it generally will, strategic behavior may prevent the parties from bargaining to the efficient output.

The damage remedy can reach the efficient outcome despite the court's imperfect information. This result can be guaranteed, however, only if the court assigns an absolute entitlement to clean air to the resident and sets liability equal to actual damages. Any other entitlement might lead to the efficient outcome but need not. For example, suppose the court assigns an intermediate entitlement to pollute to the factory corresponding to two units of output and makes the factory liable thereafter for the resident's damages. Initially, the factory would choose to produce two units since there is no liability up to and including the second unit, and liability for the third unit — equal to the resident's damages of $20,000 — exceeds the factory's additional profits — equal to $2,000. The resident would then have an incentive to "bribe" the factory to reduce output from two units to the efficient output of one unit, but because of strategic behavior the parties might not reach that output.

On the other hand, if the court chooses an entitlement corresponding to zero or one unit of output and sets liability equal to actual damages, the damage remedy will lead the factory to produce at the efficient output. In other words, with liability equal to actual damages, the damage remedy leads to

14. The alternative case in which the court knows the factory's profit schedule but not the resident's damage schedule will not be discussed because it is analogous to the present one.

the efficient outcome if, and only if, the entitlement is at or below the efficient output. However, since the court cannot determine the efficient output from its limited information, the only way it can guarantee the efficient result is to choose the entitlement corresponding to the lowest possible output — an absolute entitlement to the resident.

The discussion thus far has shown that if the court knows the victim's schedule of damages but not the injurer's schedule of profits, it generally cannot implement an efficient injunctive remedy but it can implement an efficient damage remedy. However, in many nuisance situations the court might not be able to easily determine the victim's damages. For example, although a court might be able to accurately predict the market price of someone's home, this price is generally less than the damages that would be suffered by the resident if he were forced to move, because it does not reflect the special attachment he might have for that location and house. Damages often include a subjective or idiosyncratic element of this sort that is difficult or impossible to measure.[15] We will therefore briefly reconsider the remedies when the court is assumed to underestimate the resident's damages (and, as before, to not know anything about the factory's profits). For concreteness, suppose in the example that the court's estimate of damages is $500 per unit of output.

Since the court obviously still cannot implement an efficient injunctive remedy, the discussion will focus on the damage remedy. Suppose an absolute entitlement is awarded to the resident. If damages were accurately measured, then, as we saw above, the damage remedy would lead to the efficient outcome. Now, however, with damages underestimated, the factory will generally overshoot the efficient output. In the example, with liability equal to $500 per unit of output, the factory will choose to produce three units since its additional profit from producing each unit exceeds $500 (see Table 1).

Starting at an output of three units, the resident would be better off by $19,500 if output were reduced by one unit — he would lose a $500 liability payment, but his damages would

15. In practice, this element of damages is generally excluded from a damage award.

decline by $20,000 (see Table 1). The factory would lose only $1,500 by this change — its profits would fall by $2,000, but it would avoid a $500 liability payment. Thus, if the parties could reach an agreement in which the resident paid the factory some amount between $1,500 and $19,500 to reduce output by one unit, both parties would be better off. However, because of strategic behavior, such a deal will not necessarily occur. And even if an agreement were reached with respect to this unit, the parties might fail to reach an agreement when they negotiate over reducing output from two units to the efficient output of one unit.

The general point of this discussion can be simply stated. If courts underestimate the victim's damages, then the damage remedy will lead initially to an excessive output and this inefficiency may not be corrected because of strategic behavior. There is then no general reason to believe that a damage remedy would be preferable to an injunctive remedy. For example, suppose that, starting with an absolute entitlement to the resident, the damage remedy would lead to an output of three units for the reasons described in the previous paragraph, and the injunctive remedy would lead to an output of zero units because of strategic behavior. The injunctive outcome is then more efficient than the damage outcome because total profits less total damages are $0 rather than −$20,000 (see Table 1). In general, however, either remedy could be the more efficient one.

We can now summarize the results in this chapter regarding the efficiency analysis of nuisance remedies. If the parties can be expected to bargain cooperatively (and there are no other transaction costs), then every choice of entitlement and remedy will be efficient. If the parties are likely to act strategically, then the efficient outcome can still be achieved under both remedies if the court has adequate information. Strategic behavior can be overcome under the injunctive remedy by choosing the entitlement that corresponds to the efficient outcome, which can be determined only by knowing the injurer's benefits from engaging in the harmful activity and the victim's damages. And strategic behavior can be overcome under the damage remedy by giving an absolute entitlement to the victim and setting liability equal to actual damages, which obviously requires knowledge of the victim's damages. If the court knows only the victim's damages, the injunctive remedy generally will fail because the court cannot accurately set the entitlement equal to the efficient outcome, but the damage remedy can still guarantee the efficient outcome. However, if the court underestimates the victim's damages, then the damage remedy generally will lead to excessive output and may be less desirable than the injunctive remedy.

Although either remedy could therefore be more efficient in the abstract, it may be apparent in particular circumstances that one remedy is likely to be better than the other. For example, suppose a court is confident that its estimate of the victim's damages is close to the truth, but believes that its estimate of the injurer's benefits is inaccurate. Then an entitlement to the victim protected by a damage remedy generally would be preferred because this would be likely to lead to an outcome close to the efficient solution. Alternatively, suppose a court has bad information both about the victim's damages and the injurer's benefits, but is confident that the efficiency loss from too little activity by the injurer is small relative to the efficiency loss from excessive activity. Then an entitlement to the victim protected by an injunctive remedy would be desirable because this would guarantee that the final outcome will not be too bad. Thus, the efficiency analysis of nuisance law may be helpful even when there is some uncertainty about which entitlement and remedy to choose.

CHAPTER 5

SECOND APPLICATION —
BREACH OF CONTRACT

Another area of law that can be discussed within the Coasian framework of bargaining among a small number of individuals is contract law. Unlike the normal nuisance law situation, however, the parties to a contract negotiate with each other before any dispute arises. Since the parties could decide in advance how to resolve potential disputes, it might be asked whether it is necessary or desirable to have general legal rules governing contract disputes. The reason contract rules are desirable is, of course, that it is costly to negotiate and draft a contract that provides for every conceivable contingency. For contingencies that are thought to be unlikely or that do not affect the parties' costs and benefits very much, it is not worth going to the trouble to specify in advance what to do if the contingency should occur.

Contract law can be viewed as filling in these "gaps" in the contract — attempting to reproduce what the parties would have agreed to if they could have costlessly planned for the event initially. Since the parties would have included contract terms that maximize their joint benefits net of their joint costs — both parties can be made better off if this is done — this approach is equivalent to designing contract law according to the efficiency criterion.[16]

16. The statement that the parties would have maximized their joint benefits net of their joint costs obviously presumes that they would have bargained cooperatively. Also, the conclusion that the maximization of the parties' joint benefits net of their joint costs is the goal of efficiency presumes that no one else is affected by the contract.

In this chapter, we will examine three remedies for breach of contract from this perspective. One, *expectation damages,* awards the breached-against party an amount of money that puts him in the same position he would have been in had the contract been completed. Another, *reliance damages,* awards an amount of money that puts the breached-against party in the position he would have been in had he never entered into the contract initially. The last, *restitution damages,* awards the breached-against party an amount of money corresponding to any benefits that he has conferred upon the breaching party.[17]

The analysis will be undertaken using an example in which a seller, *S,* can produce a good, called a "widget," for $150. Widgets are not generally available. For this reason, a buyer, *B1,* who values the widget at $200, enters into a contract with *S* for the future delivery of a widget. The contract price is paid in advance. In order to use the widget, *B1* must make an expenditure of $10 prior to delivery (for example, he might have to modify his warehouse slightly to store the widget). This will be referred to as his *reliance expenditure* or *reliance investment.* If the contract is not completed, this expenditure is assumed to have no value.[18]

Before delivery occurs, there is a chance that some other buyer, *B2,* may also want the widget. The value *B2* attaches to the widget is not known at the time *S* and *B1* enter into their contract. For simplicity, it is assumed that *B2's* value will turn out to be either $0, $180, or $250, and that he will offer this amount for it. Thus, after *S* and *B1* have entered into their contract, there is a chance that *B2* will offer more for the widget than *B1* did — if *B2's* value is $250. Both *S* and *B1* are assumed to be aware of these possibilities. The facts of this example are summarized in Table 2 (ignore for now the note at the bottom of the table).

17. Another remedy, liquidated damages, will be discussed in Chapter 8 below.

18. The assumptions that the contract price is paid in advance and that the reliance investment has no value in the event of breach are not essential and do not affect any of the general conclusions in this chapter.

TABLE 2

Breach of Contract Example

S is the seller:

S's cost to produce the widget is $150.

$B1$ is the initial buyer:

$B1$'s value of the widget is $200.   ·

$B1$'s reliance expenditure is $10.[a]

$B1$ pays S the contract price in advance.

$B2$ is the second buyer:

$B2$'s value of the widget is $0 or $180 or $250.

a. The possibility that $B1$ can spend an additional $24 on reliance and thereby increase the value of the widget to him by $30 is also considered.

It will also be assumed in this chapter that the parties are *risk neutral.* This means that they only care about the *expected value* of a risky situation — that is, the magnitude of a potential loss or gain multiplied by the probability of the loss or gain occurring. For example, the expected gain from a situation involving a 50 percent chance of winning $10,000 is $5,000. A risk-neutral person would, by definition, be indifferent between this situation and any other one with the same expected gain — such as a situation involving a 25 percent chance of winning $20,000, or one involving a certainty of winning $5,000.

A Fully Specified Contract

Before considering how breach of contract remedies fill in the gaps in incompletely specified contracts, it will be useful to examine the contract between S and $B1$ when everything is specified in advance. Suppose the contract has the following provisions. First, the contract price, payable in advance, is $175. Second, if the value $B2$ attaches to the widget is $0 or $180, then S is to deliver the widget to $B1$. In this case, S's profit is $25 — the contract price of $175 less S's production cost of $150 — and $B1$'s profit is $15 — the $200 value to $B1$ less his $10 reliance expenditure and less the contract price of $175. Third, the contract states that in the event that $B2$ values the widget at $250, S is to sell to $B2$ rather than $B1$, but then must pay $B1$ $225. In this case S's profit is $50 — the contract price of $175 less S's production cost of $150 plus $B2$'s payment to S of $250 less S's payment to $B1$ of $225. $B1$'s profit is then $40 — the $225 payment from S less the reliance expenditure of $10 and less the contract price paid in advance of $175.

It is clear that this fully specified contract between S and $B1$ is efficient. The only choice the parties have to make that affects their *joint* profits is whether S is to sell to $B2$ if $B2$ wants the widget. If S does not sell to $B2$, then the joint profits of S and $B1$ are $40 — S's profit of $25 plus $B1$'s profit of $15. If S does sell to $B2$ when $B2$ values the widget at $250, then the joint profits of S and $B1$ rise to $90 — S's profit of $50 plus $B1$'s profit of $40. However, if S were to sell to $B2$ when $B2$ values the widget at $180, the joint profits of S and $B1$ would fall to $20 since, together, they would have revenue of $180 and costs of $160 ($S$'s production cost of $150 plus $B1$'s reliance expenditure of $10). Thus, the provisions in the contract that call for S to sell the widget to $B2$ if $B2$ values it at $250 but not if he values it at $0 or $180 are efficient.[19]

It is important to note that there is a close relationship between the contract price and the amount of money S has to pay to $B1$ if S sells the widget to $B2$. In general, the higher the amount paid to $B1$, the higher the contract price. For example, suppose S has to pay $B1$ $240 rather than $225 in the event that the widget is sold to $B2$. $B1$ clearly would prefer to receive the higher payment in the event of a breach, and S clearly would prefer to pay the lower amount. Presumably, therefore, S will demand, and $B1$ will be willing to offer, a higher contract price in advance — say, $180 instead of $175.

---

19. Since $B2$ is assumed to offer an amount equal to the value he attaches to the widget, his profits are not affected by how valuable the widget is to him. This is why $B2$'s profits do not need to be taken into account in determining the efficient contract provisions.

Efficient Breach

Thus far, the example illustrates a simple but fundamental principle in the economic analysis of contract law: A fully specified contract is efficient. In practice, however, the cost of contracting will lead the parties to ignore relatively unimportant contingencies. Therefore, now suppose S and $B1$ do not bother to include a provision in the contract that deals with the possibility that $B2$ will offer more for the widget because they think that such an offer is unlikely. The contract simply states that S is to deliver a widget to $B1$ at some price payable in advance. We will now examine whether the expectation, reliance, and restitution remedies for breach of contract are efficient alternatives to an explicit contract provision regarding when the widget should be sold to $B2$ rather than $B1$. An important assumption in the following analysis is that if S wants to breach the contract, $B1$ will not find it worthwhile (because of bargaining costs) to attempt to stop S from breaching or to repurchase the widget from $B2$ after the breach. (If it were costless for $B1$ to negotiate with S or $B2$, then the Coasian analysis in Chapter 3 implies that every remedy would be efficient.)

First consider a breach of the contract when the expectation remedy is applicable. If the contract had been completed, $B1$ would have made a profit equal to the $200 value he places on the widget less his reliance expenditure and less the contract price he paid in advance. Thus, to put $B1$ in the same position he would have been in had the contract been completed, it is necessary to compensate $B1$ $200 (since $B1$ has already incurred the reliance expense and has paid S the contract price). Given a damage payment of $200, S will decide to breach if $B2$ offers $250 for the widget, but not if he offers $180 (or, of course, $0). Thus, the expectation remedy leads to the efficient outcome. Put differently, the expectation remedy is an efficient substitute for explicit contract provisions governing breach. It thereby saves the parties the cost and inconvenience of dealing with unlikely contingencies every time they enter into a contract. Instead, they can simply rely on a breach of contract remedy in the few instances when the issue of breach might arise.

Note that the conclusion that the expectation remedy induces efficient breach decisions does not depend on what the actual contract price is. S will have to pay B1 $200 in the event of breach regardless of the contract price since, given that B1 paid the contract price (and incurred the reliance expense) in advance, $200 is the amount of money necessary to put B1 in the same position he would have been in had the contract been completed. Thus, regardless of the contract price, S will breach in order to sell to B2 only if B2 offers more than $200 for the widget.

Next consider the reliance remedy. If B1 had not entered into the contract with S, it is assumed that he would have earned zero profit.[20] Thus, to put B1 in the same position he would have been in had he never entered into the contract, it is necessary to compensate B1 for his $10 reliance investment and to return to him the contract price that he paid in advance. In other words, the reliance measure of damages equals the reliance expenditure plus the contract price.

To determine the effects of the reliance remedy on S's decision to breach, it is therefore necessary to discuss the setting of the contract price. Since S's production cost is $150, he will not be willing to accept less than this amount. B1 will be willing to pay up to $190 for the widget since he values it at $200 but has to make the $10 reliance investment. Thus, the contract price will be somewhere between $150 and $190, the exact price depending on the relative bargaining strengths of the parties. Suppose, for concreteness, it is $160.

Given a reliance expenditure of $10 and a contract price of $160, the reliance remedy would award B1 $170 in the event of a breach by S. Therefore, S will breach the contract if B2 offers either $180 or $250 for the widget since S has to pay only $170 in damages. If B2's value is $180, the breach will be inefficient because the value B2 attaches to the widget is less than the $200 value B1 attaches to it. In other words, the reliance remedy may lead to an inefficient breach.

Finally, consider the restitution remedy. The only benefit B1 has conferred upon S has been that he paid the contract price

20. This assumption is not essential and does not affect any of the general conclusions about the reliance remedy.

in advance. Thus, to award *B1* an amount of money corresponding to the benefit he has conferred, it is necessary to force *S* to return the contract price to *B1*. In other words, restitution damages equal the contract price. For the same reasons discussed with respect to the reliance remedy, the contract price will be somewhere between $150 and $190. If it is below $180, then the restitution remedy will also lead to an inefficient breach when *B2* values the widget at $180.

In general, the restitution remedy is more likely to lead to inefficient breaches than the reliance remedy for the following reasons. First note that the contract price under the restitution remedy generally would be less than the contract price under the reliance remedy. Intuitively, this is because the seller (*S* in the example) does not have to compensate the buyer (*B1* in the example) for his reliance expenditure under the restitution remedy, but he does have to under the reliance remedy. Consequently, the buyer presumably would not be willing to pay as much for the contract under the restitution remedy, and the seller presumably would be willing to accept less. Given a lower contract price under the restitution remedy, the damage payment also would be lower under that remedy since restitution damages equal the contract price, whereas reliance damages equal the contract price plus the reliance expenditure. Thus, one would expect inefficient breaches to be more likely under the restitution remedy because of the lower damage payment.

The discussion thus far illustrates several general conclusions about the economic effects of contract law. The key result is that the expectation remedy is the only remedy that creates efficient incentives with respect to breaches of contracts. This is because the expectation remedy forces the breaching party to pay in damages the value of the good to the breached-against party. If another buyer values the good more than this, then it is efficient for that buyer to have the good. Given the expectation measure of damages, the seller will have an incentive to breach in order to obtain the higher offer. If another buyer values the good less than the original buyer, a breach is not efficient and the expectation remedy will appropriately discourage such behavior. Any other measure of damages for breach of contract generally will be inefficient. If damages exceed expectation damages, then a breach might not occur even though it would be efficient. For example, if damages were $260 in the example, then S would not breach when B2 offers $250. And if damages are below expectation damages, an inefficient breach might occur. This is the problem with the reliance remedy, since it necessarily leads to a level of damages below the expectation level. The restitution remedy is even worse because it provides less than the reliance measure of damages.

Efficient Reliance

Inducing optimal breaches of contracts is not the only problem with which contract law has to deal. Another issue of concern has to do with reliance expenditures. In the example, it was assumed that B1's reliance investment was fixed at $10. In general, this expenditure can vary, and the more spent on reliance, the more valuable the contract will be to the buyer if it is completed. For example, the buyer might be able to purchase various customized pieces of equipment, each of which is capable of transforming the widget into a more valuable final product. (Because widgets are perishable, this equipment must be obtained before delivery.) In the remainder of this chapter we will analyze how remedies for breach of contract also affect the amount invested in reliance.

In order to examine the reliance decision, the example used earlier must be made slightly more complicated. It will still be assumed that the original buyer, B1, must spend at least $10 on reliance and that the widget will be worth $200 to him if this is all that he spends. But now he will have the option of spending an *additional* $24 on reliance and thereby raising the value of the widget to him by $30. As before, if the contract is not completed, the reliance expenditure will have no value. It will also be assumed that the three values the second buyer, B2, might attach to the widget — $0, $180, or $250 — are all equally likely. The relevance of this assumption will become apparent shortly.

Although it might seem that the efficiency criterion would dictate having B1 make the additional reliance investment — since this investment seems to increase the value of the widget by $30 at a cost of only $24 — this conclusion is incorrect. The increase in value occurs only if the contract is completed and *B1* obtains the widget. But, as we have seen, it is efficient for *S* to breach the contract with *B1* in order to sell to *B2* if *B2's* value of the widget turns out to be $250. Given the assumption at the end of the previous paragraph, there is a one-in-three chance that *B2* will value the widget this much. In other words, if the breach decision is efficient, there is only a two-thirds chance that *B1* will obtain the widget. Thus, while the $24 cost of reliance is certain, the $30 benefit from reliance is uncertain. The *expected* benefit — the benefit multiplied by the probability of its realization — is only $20. It is inefficient to incur a $24 cost to obtain a $20 expected benefit.

If *S* and *B1* had been able to costlessly negotiate and draft their contract initially, they would have included a provision that specified that *B1* is not to make the additional $24 reliance investment. However, negotiating over *B1's* reliance decision is not a simple matter. For example, if it is difficult for *S* to verify how much additional benefit *B1* would obtain from the additional reliance expenditure, *B1* might be able to take advantage of *S's* imperfect information. Thus, analogously to the breach of contract decision, it is reasonable to consider the possibility that a provision regarding the reliance decision was not included in the contract. We will therefore examine whether some breach of contract remedy can serve as a substitute for this provision.

Under the expectation remedy, *B1* either will receive the widget (if the contract is performed) or be given an amount of money equivalent to the value of the widget (if the contract is breached). If *B1* spends just $10 on reliance, the widget will be worth $200 to him, so expectation damages would equal $200. If he spends an additional $24 on reliance, the widget will be worth an additional $30 to him, so expectation damages would equal $230. Thus, by spending an extra $24, he will obtain a $30 benefit either because the widget will be delivered or expectation damages will be paid. Clearly, *B1* will invest the additional $24 in reliance, an inefficient outcome for the reasons discussed above. In other words, since the expectation remedy *in effect* guarantees performance, it does not force *B1* to take into account the fact that the reliance expenditure will be worthless if the contract is breached. It therefore encourages excessive reliance investments.

Under the reliance remedy, *B1* either will receive the widget or be given an amount of money equal to his reliance expenditure plus the contract price. Thus, if the contract is performed, the extra $24 investment in reliance will have been worthwhile since it will have raised the value of the widget by $30. If the contract is breached, the extra $24 will be returned since reliance damages will be that much higher. *B1* will therefore have an incentive to spend the extra $24 on reliance since this is, in effect, an investment that has no "downside" risk but that does have "upside" potential. In other words, the reliance remedy also encourages excessive reliance expenditures.

Under the restitution remedy, *B1* either will receive the widget or be given an amount of money equal to the contract price. Unlike the expectation remedy, he is not effectively guaranteed performance, and, unlike the reliance remedy, he does not get his reliance investment back in the event of breach. *B1's* reliance expenditure is now, in effect, a risky investment with a positive payoff in the event of performance and a negative payoff in the event of breach. Therefore, in order for *B1* to determine whether it is worthwhile to spend an extra $24 on reliance, he needs to know the probabilities of performance and breach. Suppose *S* breaches only when it is efficient for a breach to occur — that is, only when *B2* values the widget at $250.[21] Given the assumption that the three values *B2* might attach to the widget — $0, $180, and $250 — are all equally likely, there is a two-thirds chance of performance and a one-third chance of breach. Thus, the *expected* benefit to *B1* of the reliance expenditure is $20 — the $30 increase in value of the widget multiplied by the probability of obtaining this value. *B1* will not spend an extra $24 in reliance to obtain this expected benefit. In other

21. The supposition that *S* breaches only when it is efficient for a breach to occur is clearly counterfactual in general under the restitution remedy. This supposition is used nonetheless because it allows the effect of the reliance remedy on the extent of the reliance investment to be illustrated most easily.

words, the restitution remedy leads to the efficient reliance investment.

This discussion of the effects of breach of contract remedies on the reliance decision illustrates several general results. The principal one is that, of the remedies considered, only the restitution remedy induces efficient reliance investments. It does this because it forces the party investing in reliance to take into account the fact that the reliance expenditure is worthless if the contract is breached.[22] The expectation remedy generally leads to too much reliance because it gives the relying party the value that would have been created by the reliance investment if the contract had been performed. The reliance remedy also generally induces excessive reliance because it reimburses the relying party for the cost of reliance in the event of breach.

Another consideration in the economic analysis of breach of contract remedies is the cost of obtaining the information needed to implement each remedy. The expectation remedy requires a court to estimate what the value of the contract would have been to the breached-against party if the contract had been completed. In many contract situations, this value may be very difficult to estimate. For example, suppose the buyer is purchasing specialized electronic inputs for the production of a newly designed home computer. The court would have to predict how profitable the new computer would have been. The restitution and reliance remedies both require knowledge of the contract price, which should be readily available. The reliance remedy also requires information about the breached-against party's reliance expenditures. Since these expenditures will have been made prior to the parties' coming to the court, it should be easier for the court to obtain this information than the information required by the expectation remedy. Thus, in general, the expectation remedy would probably be the most costly to implement, the restitution remedy would be the cheapest, and the reliance remedy would be somewhere in between.

22. The "remedy" of no damages at all would also lead to the efficient reliance investment for the same reason.

Note also that if the court incorrectly estimates the value of performance to the breached-against party, then the conclusions regarding the effects of the expectation remedy on the breach decision and on the reliance decision would have to be modified. Similarly, if the breached-against party's reliance expenditures are likely to be incorrectly determined, the conclusions regarding the effects of the reliance remedy would also have to be modified.

The discussion in this chapter has shown that, in general, there does not exist a breach of contract remedy that is efficient with respect to both the breach decision and the reliance decision. With respect to breach, the expectation remedy is ideal, whereas with respect to reliance, the restitution remedy is ideal. Thus, which remedy is best overall depends on whether the breach decision or the reliance decision is more important in terms of efficiency. For example, in the example used in this chapter an inefficient breach occurred when S sold the widget to $B2$ when $B2's$ value was $180. Since $B1$ valued the widget at $200, there was an efficiency loss of $20 from inefficient breach. Inefficient reliance occurred when $B1$ spent the additional $24 in reliance. Since the expected benefit of reliance was only $20, there was an efficiency loss of $4 from inefficient reliance. Thus, in this example the breach decision was more important than the reliance decision and therefore, on balance, the expectation remedy would be preferred.

An important assumption in the discussion in this chapter was that the parties were neutral with regard to risk. In Chapter 8 we will reconsider breach of contract remedies when the parties are assumed to be averse to risk and see that, in general, none of the remedies discussed here is ideal.

CHAPTER 6

THIRD APPLICATION —
AUTOMOBILE ACCIDENTS

In both of the applications discussed thus far — nuisance law and breach of contract — it was reasonable to consider the possibility that bargaining among the parties could lead to the efficient solution. Thus, the framework of the Coase Theorem was directly applicable to these kinds of disputes. In the next application that we will examine — automobile accidents involving pedestrians — bargaining obviously cannot lead to the efficient outcome since neither drivers nor pedestrians know in advance with whom to bargain. The Coase Theorem may be helpful nonetheless. Efficient legal rules for dealing with driver-pedestrian accidents can still be derived by imagining what rules a driver and a pedestrian would have chosen if they could have costlessly gotten together before the accident. As in the other applications, the parties would have agreed to remedies that would lead them to behave so as to maximize their joint benefits net of their joint costs.

A simple example will be used to investigate the efficiency of different legal remedies in driver-pedestrian accidents. In this example, it is assumed that drivers and pedestrians are risk neutral; the discussion will therefore be in terms of the *expected* accident cost to a pedestrian — the magnitude of the harm if an accident occurs multiplied by its probability of occurrence. It is also assumed initially that only the speed of drivers affects the pedestrians' expected harm. (The example will be extended later in this chapter to include the possibilities that the number of miles driven or the care exercised by pedestrians also can affect the expected harm.) The driver has three choices: drive rapidly,

TABLE 3

Automobile Accident Example — Driver's Care Affects Expected Accident Cost

Behavior of Driver	Total Benefit to Driver	Total Expected Accident Cost to Pedestrian	Total Benefit Minus Total Cost
Drive rapidly	$120	$100	$20
Drive moderately	$80	$40	$40
Drive slowly	$50	$20	$30

drive moderately, or drive slowly. Each choice results in some benefit to the driver and some expected accident cost to the pedestrian. The driver's benefit from driving faster might be the dollar value he places on saving time. The pedestrian's harm is also assumed to have a monetary value.[23]

The data for the example are described in Table 3. For each choice of the driver, the table lists the benefit to the driver and the expected accident cost to the pedestrian. The efficient outcome requires that the driver act so as to maximize total benefit less total cost. Given the data in Table 3, it is efficient for the driver to drive moderately. Relative to this outcome, driving rapidly is inefficient because it increases the pedestrian's expected losses by $60 while increasing the driver's benefits by only $40. And driving slowly is inefficient because it lowers the driver's benefits by $30 while lowering the pedestrian's expected losses by only $20.

The Driver's Care

We will now consider the effects on the driver's behavior of two alternative rules of liability in accident law — *strict liabil-*

23. As suggested in note 6 above and in the accompanying text, economic analysis also can be used to analyze accidents in which the harm is not equivalent to the loss of money (as is the case with pain and suffering). However, the discussion would be considerably more complicated.

ity and *negligence.* Under each, the driver will choose the action that maximizes his benefits net of his expected liability payments. Under the rule of *strict liability,* the driver will be made liable for the pedestrian's accident losses regardless of the driver's care. Thus, for each action, the driver's benefit net of his expected liability payments is the same as the last column in Table 3. The driver therefore will choose to drive moderately — the efficient outcome. In essence, the rule of strict liability induces efficient behavior because it forces the injurer — in this example, the driver — to take into account all of the adverse effects of his behavior on the victim — the pedestrian.

For the rule of strict liability to be efficient, it is generally necessary for the court to be able to obtain correct information about the victim's damages. To see why, suppose in the example that the court estimates damages to be one-half of the victim's actual damages. Then, referring to Table 3, the driver's benefits net of his expected liability payments would be $70 if he drives rapidly ($120 − $50), $60 if he drives moderately ($80 − $20), and $40 if he drives slowly ($50 − $10). He would therefore choose to drive rapidly — faster than is efficient.[24] Similarly, suppose the court estimates damages to be twice what they actually are. Then the driver's benefits net of his expected liability payments would be, respectively, −$80 ($120 − $200), $0 ($80 − $80), and $10 ($50 − $40). Thus, the driver would choose to drive slowly — too slow relative to desired driving behavior. In order to focus on other considerations, it will be assumed hereafter that the court has accurate information about the victim's damages.

Under the rule of *negligence,* the driver will be made liable for the pedestrian's accident losses only if the driver does not meet some standard of care. Suppose this standard is determined by the care that would be taken if the driver acted efficiently. In the example, this corresponds to driving moderately. Thus, the driver would be liable for the pedestrian's accident losses only if the driver chooses to drive rapidly. Therefore, if he drives rapidly his benefit net of his expected liability payments is $20 (a $120 benefit less a $100 expected liability payment). If he drives

24. For similar reasons, the driver would also generally drive faster than is efficient if, given his income or wealth, he does not expect to be able to pay the full amount of the victim's damages.

moderately, it is $80 (just the benefit since there is no liability), and if he drives slowly it is $50 (again, just the benefit). Consequently, under the rule of negligence with this standard of care, the driver will choose the efficient outcome of driving moderately. In essence, the rule of negligence leads to the efficient outcome because the injurer is induced to meet the standard of care — since liability increases from zero to the victim's damages if the standard is violated — and the standard is selected to correspond to the desired behavior.

For the rule of negligence to be efficient, it is necessary for the court to have enough information to determine the efficient outcome so that the standard of care can be chosen to correspond to it. To see why, suppose in the example that the court mistakenly believes that it is efficient for the driver to drive slowly and therefore makes this behavior the standard of care. In other words, the driver is liable for the pedestrian's losses if he drives rapidly or moderately, but not if he drives slowly. Then, referring to Table 3, the driver's benefit net of his expected liability payments is $20 if he drives rapidly ($120 − $100), $40 if he drives moderately ($80 − $40), and $50 if he drives slowly ($50 − $0). Thus, the driver would choose to drive slowly, an inefficient outcome. Similarly, if the court were to make the standard of care too lenient rather than too strict, the driver would choose to drive faster than would be efficient. In order to focus on other considerations, it will be assumed hereafter that the court has enough information to select the standard of care that corresponds to the efficient outcome.

The discussion thus far illustrates a general principle in the economic analysis of accident law: In accident situations in which the only problem is to induce the injurer to take appropriate care, both strict liability and negligence are efficient, provided that liability equals actual damages if strict liability is used and that the standard of care corresponds to the efficient outcome if negligence is used.

The Pedestrian's Care

In many accident situations, however, the problem is not just to control the injurer's behavior. In general, both the injurer and the victim can affect the probability or the magnitude of the harm. For example, a pedestrian can walk rather than run when crossing a street, or a cyclist can wear a protective helmet. When both the injurer and the victim can affect the expected harm, the problem is to induce both parties to take appropriate care. We will now reexamine the rules of strict liability and negligence with respect to this additional consideration.

To allow for the expected harm to be determined by the behavior of both the driver and the pedestrian, it is necessary to extend the example used above. It will now be assumed that the pedestrian has one choice — whether to walk or to run. If he walks, then his expected accident loss is $100 if the driver drives rapidly, $40 if the driver drives moderately, and $20 if the driver drives slowly. These are the same values used in Table 3. If the pedestrian runs, his corresponding expected accident losses are $110, $50, and $30. In other words, running is assumed to raise the expected harm by $10 regardless of the driver's behavior.[25] The data for the extended example are summarized in Table 4, where it is also assumed that the driver's benefits from driving are the same as in Table 3.

The efficient solution to the accident problem now involves a specific action by both the driver and the pedestrian. If the pedestrian walks, the problem is the same as before, and the efficient outcome with respect to the driver's behavior is for him to drive moderately. If the pedestrian runs, it can be seen from Table 4 that total benefits minus total costs also are maximized when the driver drives moderately. Thus, regardless of the pedestrian's behavior, the efficient solution involves the driver's driving moderately. Whether it is efficient for the pedestrian to walk or to run depends on the relevant costs and benefits. Running rather than walking increases the pedestrian's expected harm by $10 (regardless of the driver's behavior). It will be

25. In general, the effect of the pedestrian's care on expected accident losses would depend on the driver's behavior. For example, suppose the pedestrian's decision whether to walk or to run determines the probability of an accident, while the driver's speed determines the magnitude of the harm if an accident occurs. Then the faster the driver drives, the more the expected harm will be raised by the pedestrian's decision to run. The assumption made in the text — that running raises the expected harm by an amount that does not depend on the driver's behavior — allows for great simplification of the subsequent analysis without affecting the general conclusions.

TABLE 4

Automobile Accident Example — Driver's Care and Pedestrian's Care Affect Expected Accident Cost

Behavior of Driver	Total Benefit to Driver	Total Expected Accident Cost to Pedestrian (Depending on Pedestrian's Behavior)	Total Benefit Minus Total Cost (Depending on Pedestrian's Behavior)
Drive rapidly	$120	$100 (walks)	$20 (walks)
		$110 (runs)	$10 (runs)
Drive moderately	$80	$40 (walks)	$40 (walks)
		$50 (runs)	$30 (runs)
Drive slowly	$50	$20 (walks)	$30 (walks)
		$30 (runs)	$20 (runs)

assumed that running provides additional benefits to the pedestrian valued at $5 — for example, due to the saving of time. Thus, given these costs and benefits, the efficient solution involves the pedestrian walking.

Now reconsider the rule of strict liability. The driver's benefit net of his expected liability payments corresponds to the last column in Table 4. If the pedestrian walks, the relevant values are $20, $40, and $30, depending on whether the driver drives rapidly, moderately, or slowly. The driver therefore would choose to drive moderately. If the pedestrian runs, the corresponding values are $10, $30, and $20, and the driver also would choose to drive moderately. Thus, regardless of the pedestrian's behavior, the rule of strict liability will lead the driver to behave efficiently in this example. However, the rule of strict liability will not be efficient with respect to the pedestrian's behavior. Since the pedestrian will be fully compensated for his losses, he will ignore these losses when deciding whether to walk or to run. He will consider only the $5 extra benefit from running. The pedestrian therefore will choose to run even though running increases expected accident costs by $10.

The problem of controlling the victim's behavior under the rule of strict liability can be solved by adding a defense of *contributory negligence.* In other words, the injurer is strictly liable unless the victim is contributorily negligent. This rule will result in the desired behavior of both parties.

To see this in the example, let the standard of care applicable to the pedestrian correspond to the efficient behavior of the pedestrian — walking. Thus, if the pedestrian walks, he is not contributorily negligent, so the driver would be strictly liable. If he runs, he is contributorily negligent, so the driver would be free of liability. The pedestrian then has to bear his own losses. Thus, while running rather than walking provides benefits valued at $5, it increases the expected accident cost borne by the pedestrian from zero to $110, $50, or $30, depending on whether the driver drives rapidly, moderately, or slowly (see Table 4). Clearly, the pedestrian will choose to walk in order to avoid having to bear his own losses. Given this choice by the pedestrian, the driver will be strictly liable. We have already seen that this will lead the driver to choose to drive moderately. Thus, the rule of strict liability with a defense of contributory negligence will lead both parties to take an efficient amount of care.

Next, reconsider the rule of negligence in terms of the incentives it creates for both parties to take appropriate care. Assume, as before, that the driver is negligent only if he drives rapidly. If the pedestrian walks, the driver's benefits net of his expected liability payments are the same as discussed earlier under the negligence rule, so the driver will choose to drive moderately. If the pedestrian runs, the driver's benefits net of his expected liability payments are $10 if he drives rapidly ($120 − $110), $80 if he drives moderately ($80 − $0), and $50 if he drives slowly ($50 − $0). Thus, the driver will choose to drive moderately regardless of what the pedestrian does. Since the driver will therefore not be negligent, the pedestrian will bear his own losses. He will then compare the $5 extra benefit from running to the $10 increase in expected accident costs and therefore will choose to walk. Thus, the rule of negligence will lead both parties to take an efficient amount of care.

Note that under the negligence rule it is not necessary to add a defense of contributory negligence to get the victim to take proper precautions. If a contributory negligence defense were added, it would not affect the conclusion that both parties will take an efficient amount of care. The victim would meet the standard of care applied to him to avoid being contributorily negligent and having to bear his own losses. Given that the victim is not contributorily negligent, the injurer will meet the standard of care applied to him to avoid being negligent and having to compensate the victim for his losses.

The preceding discussion of the accident problem when both parties can affect the expected harm illustrates another general result in the economic analysis of liability rules: In accident situations in which the problem is to induce both the injurer and the victim to take appropriate care, a rule of strict liability with a defense of contributory negligence *or* a rule of negligence — with or without a defense of contributory negligence — is efficient.

The Activity-Level Issue

In many accident situations, however, expected accident losses depend not only on the care exercised by each party, but also on the extent to which each party participates in the activity that is the source of the dispute. For example, the number of driver-pedestrian accidents depends in part on how much drivers drive and on how frequently pedestrians travel by foot (rather than, say, by bus). The efficient level of participation in the dispute-creating activity is determined by comparing the benefits a party would obtain from greater participation — for example, from the greater use of one's car — to the resulting increase in expected accident costs. In general, then, the problem to be solved by liability rules is how to induce both parties to take appropriate care *and* to engage in the activity to an appropriate extent.

To examine whether the rules of strict liability and negligence will lead to the efficient level of participation in the activity, the simple version of the driver-pedestrian example — the version in which only the driver's speed affects the pedestrian's expected accident costs — will be extended to include the number of miles driven. (The more general case in which ex-

TABLE 5

Automobile Accident Example — Driver's Care and Activity Level Affect Expected Accident Cost

Behavior of Driver	Total Benefit to Driver (Depending on How Much Driver Drives)	Total Expected Accident Cost to Pedestrian (Depending on How Much Driver Drives)	Total Benefit Minus Total Cost (Depending on How Much Driver Drives)
Drive rapidly	$120 (a little)	$100 (a little)	$20 (a little)
	$140 (a lot)	$130 (a lot)	$10 (a lot)
Drive moderately	$80 (a little)	$40 (a little)	$40 (a little)
	$100 (a lot)	$70 (a lot)	$30 (a lot)
Drive slowly	$50 (a little)	$20 (a little)	$30 (a little)
	$70 (a lot)	$50 (a lot)	$20 (a lot)

pected losses also are affected by the pedestrian's care and level of participation in the activity will be discussed below.) Now suppose that expected accident costs depend not only on whether the driver drives slowly, moderately, or rapidly, but also on whether he drives "a little" or "a lot." If he drives a little, then the relevant data are assumed to be the same as in the simple version of the example — that is, the same as in Table 3. If he drives a lot, then his benefits are assumed to increase by $20 and the pedestrian's expected accident costs are assumed to rise by $30, regardless of the speed at which he drives.[26] The data for the extended example are summarized in Table 5.

Since the additional benefits from driving a lot are less than the increase in expected accident costs, the efficient solution involves the driver's driving a little. If the driver drives only a little, the problem is the same as that discussed in the simple version of the driver-pedestrian example, where it was efficient for the driver to drive moderately. Put differently, driving

26. A point analogous to the one made in note 25 above applies here.

moderately and only a little maximizes total benefits less total costs. This can be seen directly in the last column of Table 5.

Under strict liability, the driver's benefit net of his expected liability payments corresponds to the last column in Table 5. Thus, the driver will choose to drive moderately and only a little. As in the earlier versions of the driver-pedestrian example, strict liability induces the injurer to behave efficiently because it forces him to take into account the adverse effects of his behavior on the victim. The only difference now is that one relevant aspect of his behavior is the extent of his participation in the activity.

Under negligence, suppose, as in the earlier versions of the example, that the driver is negligent only if he drives rapidly. Then, if his participation in the activity corresponds to driving a little, his benefit net of his expected liability payment is $20 ($120 − $100) if he drives rapidly, $80 ($80 − $0) if he drives moderately, and $50 ($50 − $0) if he drives slowly. If he drives a lot, the comparable values are $10 ($140 − $130) if he drives rapidly, $100 ($100 − $0) if he drives moderately, and $70 ($70 − $0) if he drives slowly. The driver therefore will choose to drive a lot and to drive moderately. In other words, the negligence rule with this standard of care is efficient with respect to the injurer's care but not with respect to his level of participation in the activity.

Recall from the discussion of the negligence rule in the simple version of the driver-pedestrian example that this rule is efficient only if the standard of care corresponds to the efficient behavior of the injurer.[27] The negligence rule is not efficient in the present version of the example precisely because the standard of care does not take into account one relevant aspect of the injurer's behavior — the extent of his participation in the activity. If the standard of care were to correspond to the efficient outcome of driving moderately and only a little — so that the driver *would* be negligent if he drives a lot even if he drives moderately — then the negligence rule also would lead to the efficient outcome.

In practice, however, it is usually not feasible to include the level of participation in the activity as an aspect of the standard

27. See pp. 39-40 above.

of care. For example, it would be virtually impossible for a court to determine how many miles a particular person drives each year since that person might drive a car that is shared with other family members or he might drive different cars owned by the household. If the injurer's level of participation in the activity is omitted from the standard of care, then a negligence rule generally will lead him to participate in the activity to an excessive degree. The reason for this is straightforward. If the care he exercises meets the standard of care, he will not be liable for any damages. Therefore, in deciding how much to participate in the activity, he will consider the additional benefits from greater participation but not the increase in expected accident costs. This problem with the negligence rule was illustrated by the driver-pedestrian example. Given a standard of care based only on the driver's speed, the driver chose to meet the standard by driving moderately. But he also chose to drive a lot, exceeding the efficient level of participation in the activity.

The discussion thus far of the activity-level issue can be summarized as follows: In accident situations in which the problem is to induce the injurer both to take appropriate care and to participate in the activity at an appropriate level, strict liability is efficient. Negligence also is efficient if the standard of care encompasses both the injurer's care and his level of participation in the activity. However, if the standard does not include the injurer's activity level, then the negligence rule will lead to excessive participation in the activity. In practice, the negligence rule is likely to be inefficient for this reason.

In some accident situations, the expected accident losses may depend not only on the injurer's care and activity level, but also on the victim's care and activity level. In this more general accident situation, results analogous to those just discussed would occur. Strict liability with a defense of contributory negligence would be efficient if the standard of care applicable to the victim encompasses both the victim's care and his activity level. However, if it includes only his care, then the victim will engage in the activity to an excessive degree. Similarly, negligence would be efficient if the standard of care applicable to the injurer includes both aspects of his behavior. If it includes only his care, then he will participate in the activity too much. Thus, if it is not feasible to include either party's activity level in the standard of care, the preferred liability rule depends on whether it is more important to control the injurer's or the victim's activity level. If the injurer's activity level is of greater concern, then strict liability with a defense of contributory negligence should be used. If the victim's activity level is more important, then negligence is preferable.

The final consideration in the economic analysis of liability rules that will be discussed in this chapter is the effect of each rule on the administrative costs of resolving accident disputes. These costs depend both on the number of cases litigated and on the cost of resolving each case.[28] The negligence rule might be expected to generate less litigation than the strict liability rule for the following reason. Consider the negligence rule in an accident situation in which the injurer's care was very likely to have satisfied the standard of care. Given the cost to the victim of litigating, he might not find it worthwhile to bring an action against the injurer because of the low probability of success. Yet, under the strict liability rule, he might be willing to bring an action in this accident situation because the injurer's care is not a bar to a successful suit.

Although there may be fewer cases under the negligence rule, the administrative cost of resolving each case may well be higher than under the strict liability rule. The justification for this conclusion is easiest to see when the only problem is to induce the injurer to take appropriate care. To apply a strict liability rule, the court needs to know the victim's damages. But to apply a negligence rule, the court needs to know not only the victim's damages and the injurer's benefits at different levels of the injurer's care, in order to choose a standard of care that corresponds to the efficient outcome, but also how the injurer behaved, in order to determine whether he met the standard. (When the problem is to induce both the injurer and the victim to take appropriate care, this argument does not apply because the strict liability rule then requires a defense of contributory

28. Although the following discussion is concerned with disputes that are litigated, similar points could be made with respect to disputes that are settled after costly negotiation.

negligence to be efficient.) On balance, therefore, administrative cost considerations do not clearly favor either rule. While the negligence rule is likely to lead to fewer cases being litigated than the strict liability rule, it may well generate higher administrative costs in each case.

   This chapter has shown that in accident situations in which the only problem is to create incentives for the parties to take appropriate care, both strict liability with a defense of contributory negligence and negligence are efficient. If the problem is also to induce the parties to engage in the dispute-creating activity to an appropriate extent, then both rules are still efficient provided that the relevant standards of care — the victim's under the contributory negligence defense and the injurer's under the negligence rule — incorporate the activity-level decision of the party to whom the standard is applied. In practice, however, this is not likely to be feasible. If the standard of care refers only to the relevant party's level of care, then strict liability with a defense of contributory negligence will lead to excessive participation in the activity by the victim, and negligence will lead to excessive participation by the injurer. In many accident situations it may be apparent that one party's activity level matters more than the other's, in which case the superiority of one of the rules will be clear.

   An important assumption in the discussion in this chapter was that both drivers and pedestrians were risk neutral. When accident law is reconsidered in Chapter 9 under the assumption of risk aversion, it will be seen that strict liability and negligence are no longer both efficient even in accident situations in which only the injurer's care determines the victim's expected losses.

CHAPTER 7

RISK BEARING AND INSURANCE

In both the breach of contract and automobile accident applications, some sort of risk was present. In the contract example, there was uncertainty about the needs of the second buyer, and in the accident example, there was, implicitly, uncertainty regarding whether an accident would occur. Because of the assumption in both cases that the parties were risk neutral, risk per se did not matter.

We will now consider the generally more realistic assumption that parties are *risk averse* (at least with respect to large risks). This means that they care not only about the expected value of a risky situation but also about the absolute magnitude of the risk. For example, a risk-averse person, unlike a risk-neutral person, would not be indifferent between the certainty of winning $5,000 and a 50 percent chance of winning $10,000. The risk-averse person would, by definition, prefer the $5,000 with certainty.[29]

The Bearing of Risk

To see the value of reducing or eliminating the risk borne by risk-averse persons, consider the following situation. Suppose you have recently graduated from law school and have become an associate in a private law firm. Your first assignment is to work full-time on a case that the firm has accepted on a *contin-*

---

29. Individuals may also be risk preferring. In the example in the text, this would mean that they would prefer a 50 percent chance of winning $10,000 to the certainty of winning $5,000. This case will not be dealt with in the book.

gent fee basis — the firm will receive $80,000 at the end of the year if it wins the case and nothing otherwise. Your employer knows from previous experience that there is a 50 percent chance of winning the case. The firm proposes to pay you $80,000 for the year if you win and nothing if you lose, so your expected salary is $40,000. How much would you be willing to accept with certainty instead? Suppose you would accept as little as $30,000.

This situation provides a nice business opportunity for me. I am going to start a business with some friends in which we will bear the risks of income fluctuations of recent law school graduates who work on contingent fee cases. Here's our deal: We will pay you $35,000 with certainty if you assign to us the claim on the law firm you are working for. Suppose this deal attracts one hundred other lawyers in circumstances similar to yours. At the end of the year, we can count on approximately fifty of our claims to pay $80,000 and the rest nothing, so our expected revenue is $4 million. Since we have to pay one hundred lawyers $35,000 each, our costs are $3.5 million. Thus, our profits will be approximately $500,000. We are better off entering into this deal — although each of us is risk averse too, our risks are minimal since we can be confident that approximately fifty of our claims will pay off.[30] You are better off under this deal, too — you were willing to accept as little as $30,000 instead of bearing the risk, but you have received $35,000. Therefore, this agreement between us — which is a form of insurance — is efficient.

If it isn't already obvious, we should now identify ourselves. We are the partners in your law firm. The partners bear the risks of the firm's successes and failures, while the associates' incomes are guaranteed. This makes sense because the partners can better bear the risks of the firm — they can "average out" the results of many risky cases, and since they have more wealth, they can better absorb the risks that remain.[31]

30. Readers familiar with the basic principles of probability theory will recognize that the conclusion that our risks are minimal does not follow without some additional assumptions. It is sufficient to assume that the outcomes of the associates' cases are "independent" (in the technical statistical sense) and that each of our shares in the business is "small."

31. This statement obviously presumes that the higher a person's wealth, the less averse he is to a given size risk. This is a standard assumption in the economic analysis of risk.

The preceding discussion has been about a beneficial risk — that is, a risk that someone would voluntarily accept. For such risks, a risk-averse person is willing to settle for less than the expected value of the risk. In the law firm example, rather than accept the risk of an equal chance of winning $80,000 or nothing, with an expected benefit of $40,000, the associate was willing to accept as little as $30,000 with certainty. Similarly, for an undesirable risk — a risk that someone would not voluntarily accept — a risk-averse person would be willing to pay more than the expected value of the risk to avoid it. For example, consider a risk involving an equal chance of losing $80,000 or nothing, thus having an expected loss of $40,000. A risk-averse person might be willing to pay as much as $45,000 with certainty to avoid this risk.

Since risk-averse individuals are willing to pay for the reduction of risk, just as they are willing to pay for more tangible commodities, the benefit from eliminating or reducing the risk borne by such individuals is properly included in the efficiency calculus. A natural way to measure this benefit is to compare the expected value of the risk and, in the case of a beneficial risk, the least amount of money the person would accept with certainty instead, or, in the case of a detrimental risk, the greatest amount of money the person would pay to avoid the risk. In the law firm example, the expected value of the risk was $40,000, while the associate was willing to accept as little as $30,000 with certainty. Thus, the benefit of removing the risk was $10,000. In the example of a detrimental risk at the end of the previous paragraph, the value of removing the risk was $5,000 since the risk-averse person was willing to pay $45,000 with certainty to avoid a risk with an expected loss of $40,000.

Insurance

One common way of eliminating risk is through insurance. For detrimental risks, the insured person pays some amount of money with certainty — the insurance premium — in return for which he is fully compensated if the undesirable risk materializes. For beneficial risks, the insured person receives some amount of money with certainty in return for allowing someone else to benefit from the desirable outcome if it occurs, as in the law firm example. This, too, may be thought of as a form of insurance.

An insurance policy that completely eliminates the risk might, however, have an undesirable side effect. In the law firm example, the associate will have less of an incentive to work hard in order to win the case if his income for the year does not depend on his winning the case. This kind of problem also arises with respect to undesirable risks. For example, if personal items left in your car are completely insured against theft, you may be more likely to leave your camera on the back seat rather than to go to the trouble of putting it in the trunk. These two examples illustrate a general problem — the provision of insurance may increase the probability of a loss or the size of the loss because the insured person has less of an incentive to take precautions. In the insurance literature this phenomenon is called the problem of *moral hazard.*

In principle, the moral hazard problem can be overcome by adjusting the insurance premium to reflect the increase in the expected loss resulting from the insured person's taking less care. For example, suppose your camera is worth $500 and that putting it in the trunk of your car eliminates the possibility of theft, whereas leaving it on the back seat leads to a one-in-a-hundred chance of having it stolen. In other words, leaving it on the back seat leads to an *expected* loss of $5. If your insurance premium were to increase by $5 if you regularly left your camera on the back seat of your car, then you would leave it there only if it is worth at least $5 to you to do so. It may or may not be worth this much to leave it there. For example, if you are a professional photographer specializing in outdoor photography, it probably would be worth paying $5 more for the extra convenience, whereas for most people the added convenience would not be worth this much. In either case, by being forced to pay more because of the increased expected loss, the insured person will have the appropriate incentive to take precautions. In other words, the moral hazard problem can be eliminated if the insurance premium is based on the care exercised by the insured person.

This solution to the moral hazard problem usually is not feasible in practice because the insurer cannot cheaply monitor the behavior of the person being insured. In the camera example, an ideal insurance policy would require that the insurance company determine whether the insured person regularly left his camera on the back seat of his car. In the law firm example, monitoring is easier, and, as a result, bonuses and promotions can be used to some extent to encourage effort (with some resulting imposition of risk).

There are other alternatives in practice to monitoring the insured person's behavior and adjusting the premium accordingly. In general, these alternatives involve providing only partial insurance in order to induce the insured person to take some precautions. Sometimes this takes the form of a *deductible*, in which, for example, the insured person bears the first $100 of loss and the insurance company bears the rest. Other times it takes the form of *co-insurance*, in which, for example, the insured person bears 20 percent of all losses. In either case, this approach is obviously a compromise since it leaves some risk on a risk-averse person and, in general, it will not completely solve the problem of moral hazard. On balance, however, partial insurance may be preferable both to no insurance at all (which leaves the most risk on risk-averse persons) and to complete insurance (which provides little or no incentive to take precautions).

The discussion in this chapter has shown that the elimination or reduction of risk borne by a risk-averse person is a benefit that should be taken into account in applying the efficiency criterion. One common way in which risk is reduced is through insurance. An ideal insurance policy has two features — it provides full coverage in order to eliminate the bearing of risk, and it bases the premium on the behavior of the insured person in order to eliminate the problem of moral hazard. In practice, however, it is often difficult to monitor the insured person's behavior; consequently, insurance is likely to be less than complete in order to improve the insured person's incentive to take precautions.

We will now return to the breach of contract and automobile accident applications and reexamine them in light of these principles of risk bearing and insurance. The contract application illustrates the case of a beneficial risk (the uncertainty of a higher third-party offer), while the accident application obviously represents the case of a detrimental risk.

CHAPTER 8

FOURTH APPLICATION —
BREACH OF CONTRACT AGAIN

In the discussion of breach of contract in Chapter 5, it was assumed that the parties were risk neutral. The primary conclusions there were that the expectation remedy was most efficient with respect to the breach decision and that the restitution remedy was most efficient with respect to the reliance decision. We will now reexamine breach of contract remedies when at least one of the parties is risk averse. In order to focus on the risk-allocation issue, assumptions will be made that imply that both the breach decision and the reliance decision will be efficient under all of the remedies considered.

The analysis will be undertaken using a variation of the earlier example of a seller, S, who can produce a widget for $150, an initial buyer, B1, who values the widget at $200 and who has to make a reliance investment of $10, and a possible second buyer, B2. The contract price between S and B1 is again payable in advance.[32] It is assumed in this chapter that B1's reliance expenditure is fixed, so there cannot be a problem of inefficient reliance. It is also assumed that the value B2 attaches to the widget will turn out to be either $0 or $250. The facts of this example are summarized in Table 6 (which is a slightly modified version of Table 2).

By eliminating the possibility considered earlier that B2's value might also be $180, the problem of inefficient breach is

_____

32. Although none of the results in this chapter depends on the specific contract price, it will be useful to keep in mind that the contract price varies with the damage payment for the reasons discussed in Chapter 5. See p. 28 above.

TABLE 6

Breach of Contract Example

S is the seller:

  S's cost to produce the widget is $150.

B1 is the initial buyer:

  B1's value of the widget is $200.

  B1's reliance expenditure is $10.

  B1 pays S the contract price in advance.

B2 is the second buyer:

  B2's value of the widget is $0 or $250.

avoided under all of the remedies examined; this can be explained as follows. It was shown in Chapter 5 that the level of damages under the remedies considered was at least as large as the contract price (this was the level of damages under the restitution remedy), but no greater than the $200 value B1 attaches to the widget (the level of damages under the expectation remedy).[33] Consequently, if B2 does not need the widget, S obviously will not breach, while if B2's offer is $250, S will breach in order to sell to B2 *regardless of which remedy is used.* In other words, the breach decision will be efficient under all of the remedies considered. Thus, since the reliance expenditure is fixed and the breach decision is efficient, the only issue to be discussed is risk allocation.

Optimal Risk Allocation

Since it will be assumed throughout this chapter that private insurance is not available to the parties, the allocation of contract risks will be determined solely by the remedy for breach of contract. Before examining the effects of different

33. See pp. 29-31 above.

remedies, it will be useful to determine the level of damages that would be awarded in the widget example if the risk were allocated efficiently or optimally. Suppose for a start that the buyer, *B1*, is risk averse and that the seller, *S*, is risk neutral.[34] Then, since it is desirable to eliminate the risks imposed on risk-averse persons, *B1* should, in effect, be insured, and *S* should bear all of the risk. This can be accomplished by making *S* pay *B1* in the event of a breach an amount of money equal to the value *B1* attaches to the widget — that is, $200. Given this damage payment, *B1's* profit equals his $200 benefit less the contract price and less his $10 reliance expenditure regardless of whether *B2's* offer materializes and *S* breaches. *S's* profit, however, does depend on whether *B2's* offer occurs. If the offer does not occur, *S's* profit equals the contract price less his $150 production cost, whereas if it does occur, his profit is augmented by $50 — the difference between *B2's* $250 offer and the $200 damage payment to *B1*. Thus, with this damage payment, *B1* does not bear any risk but *S* does.

Now suppose that *S* is risk averse and *B1* is risk neutral. Then *S* should be insured and all of the risk should be borne by *B1*. This can be achieved by making *S* pay *B1* if a breach occurs an amount of money equal to *B2's* offer — that is, $250. *S's* profit then equals the contract price less his $150 production cost regardless of whether the contract is performed or breached since, in the event of a breach, he must disgorge the extra profits he otherwise would have obtained from the sale to *B2*. *B1's* profit equals his $200 value less the contract price and less his $10 reliance expenditure if the contract is performed, or the $250 damage payment less the contract price and reliance expenditure if the contract is breached. Thus, only *B1's* profit is uncertain.

Finally, if both *B1* and *S* are risk averse, the risk should be shared between them in a way that reflects their relative aversion to risk. This can be accomplished by a damage payment

34. Recall from note 19 above that *B2* is assumed to offer an amount equal to the value he attaches to the widget, so his profits do not depend on how valuable the widget is to him. In other words, *B2* does not bear any risk. This is why it does not matter in the example whether *B2* is risk neutral or risk averse.

between the two extremes discussed above — that is, between *B1's* value of $200 and *B2's* offer of $250. To the extent that the damage payment is above $200, *B1* bears the risk of a higher offer since the difference between *B1's* profit when the contract is performed and *B1's* profit when the contract is breached increases. Similarly, to the extent that the damage payment is below $250, *S* bears this risk because *S's* profit becomes more uncertain. Thus, the more risk averse *B1* is relative to *S*, the lower the optimal damage payment. Note, however, that the optimal damage payment is never below the $200 value *B1* attaches to the widget. It equals this value only when *B1* is risk averse and *S* is risk neutral.

The Effects of the Remedies

We can now reexamine the expectation, reliance, and restitution remedies to see whether, and under what circumstances, they optimally allocate the contract risks in the example. Under the expectation remedy, if the seller breaches, the buyer can recover from the seller an amount of money that puts the buyer in the same position he would have been in had the contract been completed. As seen in Chapter 5, this corresponds in the example to a damage payment equal to the $200 value *B1* attaches to the widget.[35] *B1's* profit therefore does not depend on whether *S* breaches to sell the widget to *B2*, but *S's* profit does. In other words, the beneficial risk of *B2's* offer is borne entirely by *S*; *B1* is in effect completely insured against this risk. Based on the earlier discussion of optimal risk allocation, we can conclude, therefore, that the expectation remedy is efficient in terms of risk allocation only if the seller is risk neutral and the buyer is risk averse.

Under the reliance remedy, the buyer can recover an amount of money that puts him in the same position he would have been in had he never entered into the contract with the seller. It was seen in Chapter 5 that reliance damages correspond in the example to *B1's* $10 reliance expenditure plus the con-

35. See pp. 29-30 above.

tract price; it was also demonstrated that this level of damages was necessarily less than the level of expectation damages — that is, less than the $200 value *B1* attaches to the widget.[36] Recall from the discussion of optimal risk allocation earlier in this chapter that the optimal damage payment is never below the $200 value *B1* attaches to the widget and that it is only this low when *B1* is risk averse and *S* is risk neutral. Thus, the reliance remedy never leads to the optimal allocation of the contract risk in this example. Intuitively, this is because the effect of the reliance remedy is to accentuate the risk created by the possibility of a third-party offer. The further the damage payment falls below *B1's* value of the widget, the greater the variability of both *B1's* profit and *S's* profit.

Under the restitution remedy, the buyer can recover any benefit that he has conferred upon the seller. It was shown in Chapter 5 that restitution damages correspond in the example to the contract price, which will be below *B1's* $200 value.[37] Thus, the restitution remedy, like the reliance remedy, would never optimally allocate the contract risk because the damage payment would always be too low.

The preceding discussion illustrates a general conclusion about the risk-allocation effects of breach of contract remedies: When the contract risk is due to the possibility of a third-party offer, the expectation remedy is ideal when the buyer is risk averse and the seller is risk neutral. Moreover, it is preferable to both the reliance and the restitution remedies (regardless of the parties' relative aversion to risk).

In many contract situations, however, the seller may be risk averse and the buyer may be risk neutral, in which case the parties would want the buyer to bear the risk; or both parties may be risk averse, in which case they would want to share the risk rather than to allocate it entirely to one party. Then the expectation remedy is not ideal. However, there is an alternative — a *liquidated damage* remedy — that can effectively allocate the contract risk between the parties in any way they desire. Under a liquidated damage remedy, if the seller breaches, the

36. See p. 30 above.
37. See pp. 30-31 above.

buyer can recover an amount of money agreed to by the parties in advance. This remedy differs from the others in that it is arranged by the parties themselves before a breach has occurred or been attempted. If their only concern is with the allocation of risk, as has been assumed throughout this chapter, then they would choose a damage payment that allocates the risk according to their relative aversion to risk. In principle, then, a liquidated damage remedy would always allocate the contract risk optimally because the liquidated damage payment would equal the optimal damage payment.[38]

To see how a liquidated damage remedy allocates contract risks, suppose in the example that S and B1 are equally risk averse and therefore want to split the beneficial risk of a higher offer from B2. This can be done by the completely specified contract discussed in Chapter 5, which had the following provisions. B1 pays S the contract price of $175 in advance. If B2's needs do not materialize, then S is to deliver the widget to B1. If B2 does need the widget, then S is to sell the widget to B2 (for $250) rather than to B1 but must then pay B1 liquidated damages of $225. Under this arrangement, S's profit is $25 if B2 does not need the widget ($175 − $150) and $50 if B2 does need it ($175 − $150 + $250 − $225). Similarly, B1's profit is $15 if B2 does not need the widget ($200 − $175 − $10, where the last item is B1's reliance expenditure) and $40 if B2 does need it ($225 − $175 − $10). Note that the joint profits of S and B1 rise by $50 if B2 needs the widget — from joint profits of $40 ($25 + $15) if B2 does not need the widget to joint profits of $90 ($50 + $40) if he does. The liquidated damage remedy allocates half of this beneficial risk to each party — both S's and B1's profits rise by $25 in the event that B2 needs the widget. Note, in contrast, that the expectation remedy would allocate all of the risk to S — S's profits would rise by $50 if B2 needs the widget whereas B1's profits would not change.

This example is illustrative of a more general point: A liquidated damage remedy can allocate the contract risks be-

38. In practice, however, courts generally will not enforce a liquidated damage agreement unless the liquidated damage payment is a reasonable approximation of the expectation measure of damages. If the liquidated damage payment is larger, it is said to be an unenforceable "penalty."

tween the parties according to their relative aversion to risk. Thus, in terms of risk allocation, a liquidated damage remedy is equivalent to the expectation remedy when the buyer is risk averse and the seller is risk neutral, and it is preferable to the expectation remedy when the opposite is true or when both parties are risk averse. Note, however, that a liquidated damage remedy requires, relative to the other remedies, additional negotiation by the parties when they enter into the contract since they must also decide on the amount of the payment in the event of a breach. Thus, the potential benefits of a liquidated damage remedy in terms of risk allocation must be balanced against the additional cost of contract negotiation. If the risk allocation benefits do not justify incurring this extra cost, then a court-imposed remedy, such as the expectation remedy, would be preferable.

   The discussion in this chapter reinforces the conclusion in Chapter 5 that there does not exist a breach of contract remedy that is efficient with respect to every consideration. It was shown there that the expectation remedy is preferred with respect to the breach decision and that the restitution remedy is preferred with respect to the reliance decision. And we have seen here that a liquidated damage remedy is generally preferred with respect to risk allocation. Thus, which remedy is best overall depends on the relative importance of these three considerations in each contract situation, or type of contract situation.

   It may turn out, however, that one remedy clearly dominates the others in a particular type of contract situation. For example, consider contracts in which the sellers of a good each supply many buyers. Then it might be presumed that the sellers are risk neutral since they can, in effect, "self-insure." Suppose also that the buyers do not have to undertake any reliance investments prior to receiving the good. Then the expectation remedy would be ideal in these types of contracts. It would induce efficient breach decisions, allocate the contract risks to a risk-neutral party, and not distort the buyer's reliance decision.

CHAPTER 9

FIFTH APPLICATION —
AUTOMOBILE ACCIDENTS AGAIN

In the earlier discussion of automobile accidents, it was assumed that the injurer (the driver) and the victim (the pedestrian) were neutral with respect to risk. One of the principal conclusions there was that both strict liability and negligence are efficient if the only problem is to induce the injurer to take appropriate care. We will now reexamine these remedies when the parties may be averse to risk. We will also consider the relevance of insurance to the accident problem. If risk allocation is a consideration, it no longer will be true that both liability rules are efficient even when the only other issue is the control of the injurer's care.

The discussion will be based on the simple version of the driver-pedestrian example described in Chapter 6 — that is, the version in which the victim's expected harm is determined solely by the driver's speed. (To consider the possibility that the driver's activity level or the victim's care or activity level can also affect the expected harm would greatly complicate the discussion of the interaction between liability rules, risk allocation, and insurance without adding much additional insight.) The data for the simple version of the driver-pedestrian example were contained in Table 3, which is reproduced here as Table 7. That table included the *expected* accident cost to the pedestrian but did not explain how it was derived from the underlying probability and magnitude of the loss. This omission was irrelevant because it was assumed that the parties were risk neutral; by definition, they cared only about the expected outcome. Now, however, given the assumption that they may be risk

TABLE 7

Automobile Accident Example — Driver's Care Affects Expected Accident Cost

Behavior of Driver	Total Benefit to Driver	Total Expected Accident Cost to Pedestrian	Total Benefit Minus Total Cost
Drive rapidly	$120	$100	$20
		(= $10,000 × 1/100)	
Drive moderately	$80	$40	$40
		(= $10,000 × 1/250)	
Drive slowly	$50	$20	$30
		(= $10,000 × 1/500)	

averse, not only does the expected value of the loss matter, but so does the particular probability and magnitude of the loss. Suppose, for concreteness, that the loss if an accident occurs is $10,000[39] and that the probability of an accident is 1/100 if the driver drives rapidly, 1/250 if he drives moderately, and 1/500 if he drives slowly. These numbers are included in Table 7 below the expected accident cost data.

Private Insurance Not Available

We will first consider the accident problem when private insurance is not available to either party. This assumption may be realistic in some circumstances. For example, because of the administrative cost of running an insurance company, the premium charged might have to be so high that risk-averse persons would not be willing to buy insurance at that price. Consequently, no company would be able to remain in business.

Since we are assuming that only the driver's behavior affects the expected accident loss, only the rules of strict liability and

39. Recall the assumption that all losses are monetary. But see note 23 above.

negligence need to be considered. Under strict liability, although neither party can buy private insurance, the pedestrian is in effect insured since, whenever an accident occurs, the driver must compensate the pedestrian for his full damages of $10,000. Thus, under this rule, the risk of an accident is borne entirely by the driver.[40]

Under the rule of negligence, the driver will be liable only if he does not meet the standard of care. Assuming that he does meet it — for the reasons discussed in Chapter 6[41] — he will not be liable and therefore the pedestrian will have to bear his own losses. Thus, under the negligence rule, the risk of an accident is borne entirely by the pedestrian.

This discussion shows that the rules of strict liability and negligence allocate the accident risks in completely asymmetrical ways. These risk-allocation effects did not matter in terms of efficiency in our initial discussion of automobile accidents in Chapter 6 because both parties were assumed to be risk neutral. If, however, one party is risk averse and the other is risk neutral, then there is a clear preference for one liability rule. When the pedestrian is the risk-averse party, the rule of strict liability leads to the ideal allocation of risks, whereas if the driver is the risk-averse party, the rule of negligence results in ideal risk allocation.

In many accident situations, however, both parties may be risk averse. It would therefore be desirable in terms of risk allocation to share the risks rather than, as under the strict liability and negligence rules, to allocate them entirely to one party. This can be accomplished by modifying the strict liability rule. Rather than setting the driver's liability equal to the pedestrian's losses, as is usually done under strict liability, liability can be set lower than the actual losses, thereby leaving some of the accident risk on the pedestrian. For example, suppose the driver and the pedestrian are equally risk averse, so that the optimal allocation of the risk would be to share it equally. This allocation will result under strict liability if the driver is made liable for one-half of the pedestrian's loss — $5,000 rather than

40. This statement obviously presumes that the driver has adequate resources with which to compensate the pedestrian. If he does not, then some of the risk will remain on the pedestrian.
41. See pp. 39-40 above.

$10,000 — every time an accident occurs. Clearly, any other allocation of the risk between the two parties can be achieved by appropriately setting the level of liability somewhere between zero and the pedestrian's actual loss. Recall from Chapter 6, however, that if liability is less than the pedestrian's actual damages, the driver will generally take less than the efficient amount of care.[42] Thus, if both parties are risk averse and insurance is not available, there may be a tradeoff between the desired allocation of the risk and the desired behavior of the driver.

Ideal Insurance Available

Although the preceding discussion shows that, if both parties are averse to risk, the existing risk can be shared in the best possible way by a version of strict liability, this is less desirable than removing the risk from the parties altogether, as by private insurance. We will now consider the accident problem when *ideal* private insurance is available to both parties — liability insurance to the driver and first-party accident insurance to the pedestrian. Recall from Chapter 7 that an ideal insurance policy would provide full coverage in order to remove all risk from the insured person; it would also charge that person a premium for the insurance that reflects the expected losses resulting from his behavior, to avoid the so-called moral hazard problem.[43]

Under the strict liability rule, the pedestrian does not have any need to purchase insurance since he is effectively insured by the driver. The driver, however, will purchase a liability insurance policy with complete coverage. The insurance company's expected payout to the driver will equal the driver's expected liability payments, which are determined by the driver's behavior. Thus, given the data in Table 7, the premium charged by the insurance company will be $100 if the driver drives rapidly, $40 if he drives moderately, and $20 if he drives slowly.[44] Con-

42. See p. 39 above.
43. See pp. 53-55 above.
44. This statement implicitly assumes that there are no administrative costs of running the insurance company, and that the company just breaks even — that is, has enough premium revenue to just cover its claim payouts. The break-even assumption would be appropriate, for example, if the insurance industry is competitive and in long-run equilibrium; see pp. 85-87 below.

fronted with this premium structure the driver will choose to drive moderately since, relative to this choice, driving rapidly leads to a $60 increase in his insurance premium and to only a $40 increase in his benefits, and driving slowly lowers his benefits by $30 while lowering his insurance premium by only $20 (see Table 7). Thus, strict liability combined with ideal insurance is efficient both with respect to the care exercised by the driver and the removal of risk from both parties.

Under the negligence rule, the driver would want to buy liability insurance only if he chooses to drive rapidly, since he would not be liable otherwise. The liability insurer would charge the driver a premium of $100 in these circumstances. Faced with this premium if he drives rapidly and no liability otherwise, the driver will choose to drive moderately since the cost of the insurance policy exceeds the extra benefits from driving rapidly. Thus, the pedestrian will bear his own losses and will purchase a first-party accident insurance policy with full coverage. Given the driver's decision to drive moderately, the pedestrian's expected accident losses are $40, so this will be the premium charged. Because the pedestrian is assumed not to be able to affect the probability or magnitude of the harm, there is no possibility of moral hazard. Thus, negligence combined with ideal insurance also is efficient both with respect to the care exercised and the removal of risk.

Imperfect Insurance Available

This analysis shows that when ideal insurance is available, it does not matter whether strict liability or negligence is used in the example under consideration. However, for reasons discussed in Chapter 7, it is not realistic in many, if not most, circumstances to assume that ideal insurance is available: Because of the difficulty or impossibility of monitoring the insured person's behavior, the insurance premium will not respond completely to changes in that behavior. As a result, the insured person will not have an adequate incentive to take precautions that reduce the expected losses. This is the problem of moral hazard. Consequently, the insurance policy may not provide full coverage in order to induce the insured person to take more care. We will therefore complete the discussion of the accident problem by considering the optimal choice of a liability rule when insurance is imperfect because of the moral hazard problem. For simplicity, it will be assumed that the insurer cannot observe the insured person's behavior at all.[45]

Under the rule of strict liability, the driver will want to purchase liability insurance. If the policy provides complete coverage, the driver will have no incentive to take care since, by assumption, the premium cannot be made to depend on the driver's care. Thus, the driver would choose to drive rapidly. Alternatively, the policy may provide less than full coverage to create some incentive for the driver to drive more slowly. In either case, an ideal outcome will not be achieved under the rule of strict liability. If the coverage is complete, the driver will not exercise appropriate care, and if the coverage is incomplete, he will bear some risk (and generally still will not take enough care).

Under the negligence rule, the driver will want liability insurance only if he chooses to drive rapidly, since he would not be liable for the pedestrian's damages otherwise. If he drives rapidly, the insurance premium would be $100. Given this premium if he drives rapidly and no liability otherwise, the driver will choose to drive moderately. Note that this is the outcome that occurred when ideal insurance was assumed to be available. The fact that the liability insurer now cannot monitor the driver's care is irrelevant because the driver will meet the standard of care and therefore will not be liable.[46] Given the

45. Since individuals who take less care are more likely to have accidents, an insurance company can indirectly obtain some information about the insured person's behavior from the number of claims submitted. (If the premium charged depends on the number of claims previously paid, the policy is said to be "experience rated.") There may also be some ways to directly monitor the insured person's behavior. For example, many companies providing automobile insurance request information about the number of miles driven annually.

46. Note that this argument implicitly assumes that, although the insurance company cannot monitor the driver's care before the accident, the court can determine the driver's care after an accident. It might therefore be asked why the insurance company cannot also determine the driver's care *after* an accident. If the company could, this would not affect the discussion in the text because the driver will not have a need for insurance, given his decision to drive moderately.

driver's behavior, the pedestrian will bear his own losses and will want a first-party accident insurance policy with full coverage. Since, by assumption, there is nothing the pedestrian can do to affect the probability or magnitude of the loss, there is no moral hazard problem and therefore no reason to deny full coverage to the pedestrian. Thus, under the negligence rule, the driver will exercise appropriate care and bear no risk, and the pedestrian will be fully insured — the efficient solution. In summary then, when there is a moral hazard problem with respect to the injurer's behavior but not with respect to the victim's behavior, the negligence rule is preferable to the strict liability rule.

The discussion in this chapter has shown that considerations of risk allocation may provide a reason for adopting one automobile accident remedy rather than another. For example, if insurance is not available, we saw in the simple version of the driver-pedestrian example that the strict liability rule is preferred when the victim is risk averse and the injurer is risk neutral, and that the negligence rule is superior when the opposite is true. A modification of the strict liability rule — with liability less than the victim's actual losses — is best with respect to risk allocation when both parties are risk averse, but it generally will lead the injurer to take too little care. If ideal insurance is available to both parties, then the strict liability rule and the negligence rule are both efficient. And if, somewhat more realistically, imperfect insurance is available to the injurer because of the moral hazard problem but perfect insurance is available to the victim, then the negligence rule is efficient but the strict liability rule is not. Obviously, if the simple version of the driver-pedestrian example is not descriptive of the accident situation — that is, if the injurer's activity level or the victim's care or activity level also matter — the specific conclusions in this chapter would have to be modified. However, the basic observations developed here about the interaction between liability rules, risk allocation, and insurance would carry over to other accident situations.

CHAPTER 10

SIXTH APPLICATION —
LAW ENFORCEMENT

All of the applications thus far — nuisance law, breach of contract, and automobile accidents — have been concerned with the choice of legal rules to govern disputes in which one party to the dispute (the victim) brings an action against the other party (the injurer) to enforce the rule. In many areas of law, however, the victim is not relied upon to do the enforcing, at least not exclusively. For example, laws governing activities such as speeding or double parking, polluting the air, evading taxes, littering a highway, and attempting to monopolize an industry are enforced by public agencies instead of, or in addition to, private parties. Thus, to complement the discussions of the previous applications, this chapter will focus on the extent to which laws should be enforced, rather than on the choice of the rules themselves. As will be seen, risk-bearing considerations will also play a central role in this discussion.

The economic analysis of law enforcement will be undertaken through an example concerned with the control of double parking. Imagine a city, called Econville, in which each of the several million residents owns a car. (Econville obviously is situated in California.) Since on-street parking is often very difficult to find in Econville, residents occasionally double-park. This practice disrupts the flow of traffic and thereby imposes costs on other Econville drivers in the form of annoyance and lost time. The total cost imposed on other drivers is assumed to be $10 for each incident of double parking.

The benefits from double parking depend on the circumstances leading to the decision to double-park. These benefits might be relatively low — below $10 — if, for example, double parking allows someone to save a couple of minutes while running into a grocery store to buy a gallon of ice cream. Or these benefits might be relatively large — above $10 — if, for example, double parking allows someone to save several minutes while running into a drugstore to obtain an urgently needed medicine. It is assumed that, of the several million residents in Econville, only 100,000 residents each year obtain benefits from double parking that exceed the $10 cost created by double parking.

As the above discussion suggests, some double-parking incidents in Econville are efficient — those in which the benefits from double parking exceed the $10 congestion cost imposed on others. All other instances of double parking are inefficient. Thus, ideally, there would be only 100,000 double-parking incidents in Econville each year, those involving residents whose benefit from double parking exceeds $10.

To attempt to achieve this result, the City Council of Econville is considering instituting a fine for double parking and hiring inspectors to detect violators. The highest feasible fine that can be imposed on a double-parking violator equals the wealth of that individual. It is assumed that each Econville resident has wealth of $10,000, so this is the maximum possible fine for double parking. The cost of a full-time inspector is assumed to be $50,000 per year (including the cost of his car, gas, etc.). For simplicity, it is assumed that the City Council has only three options with respect to the number of inspectors who can be hired. If ten inspectors are hired at a total cost of $500,000 per year, every double-parking violation will be detected. If one inspector is hired at a cost of $50,000 per year, one out of every ten violators will be caught. And if one inspector is hired on a very limited basis — one day every three months — at a cost of $500 per year, one out of every thousand violations will be detected. These options are summarized in the first two columns of Table 8 (ignore for now the remaining columns).

The City Council must decide both how much to spend on enforcement — choosing from among the three options — and, given the resulting probability of detection, how high to set the fine. It will be assumed that the City Council is interested in the most efficient system of law enforcement. This means that it

TABLE 8

Law Enforcement Example — Residents Risk Neutral

Total Enforcement Costs	Probability of Detection	Fine	Expected Fine
(1)	(2)	(3)	(4)
$500,000	1.0	$10	$10
$50,000	.1	$100	$10
$500	.001	$10,000	$10

will want to deter inefficient double-parking violations — those in which the benefit from the violation is less than the $10 cost — but not efficient violations, and that it will want to achieve this outcome at the least possible cost.

The Risk-Neutral Case

For reasons that will become apparent, the efficient system of law enforcement depends on whether the residents of Econville are risk neutral or risk averse. Suppose they are all neutral with respect to risk — they care only about expected outcomes. Then, in deciding whether to double-park, a resident of Econville will compare his benefit from double parking to the expected fine — the fine multiplied by the probability of detection. Therefore, to achieve optimal deterrence — that is, deterrence only of those double-parking violations in which the benefits are less than the $10 congestion cost — it is necessary for the expected fine to equal $10. If the expected fine were larger than $10, some double-parking incidents in which the benefit exceeded the cost would be deterred, and if it were less than $10, some violations in which the benefit was less than the cost would nonetheless occur.

Given each possible expenditure on enforcement and the resulting probability of detection, the fine can be set at some level such that the *expected* fine equals $10. To see this, refer again to Table 8. If detection is certain, then the fine should be $10. If the probability of detection is .1, then a $100 fine will result in a $10 expected fine. And if the probability of detection is .001, a fine of $10,000 is necessary to generate an expected fine of $10. Thus, if the fine is set appropriately, the optimal deterrence of double-parking violations can be achieved with each expenditure on enforcement.

This observation immediately suggests what the optimal system of law enforcement is for Econville. Since the optimal deterrence of double-parking violations can be achieved with any of the three expenditures on enforcement, there is no reason not to spend the least amount possible. In other words, the City Council should hire a part-time inspector for $500 per year, catch one out of every thousand violators, and fine each violator $10,000. Since the expected fine is $10, only those individuals who gain more than this amount will double-park, and the City Council will have achieved this result at the least possible cost.

This example illustrates a basic principle in the economic analysis of law enforcement, which was first formalized by Gary Becker:[47] If individuals are risk neutral, then the efficient system of law enforcement is one in which the fine is as large as possible — equal to the wealth of the individuals whose behavior is being controlled. This allows the probability of detection to be very low in order to save enforcement costs.[48] Note that the logic of this result does not depend on the magnitude of the costs imposed on others by the harmful activity. Thus, for example, if some activity imposed only a $1 cost on others, it would still be efficient to use as large a fine as possible — $10,000 in the example — in order to achieve optimal deterrence with the smallest possible expenditure on enforcement.

Obviously, this result is not descriptive of actual enforcement policies. Individuals are rarely, if ever, fined an amount approximating their wealth, especially for engaging in activities

47. Gary S. Becker, Crime and Punishment: An Economic Approach, 76 J. Pol. Econ. 169 (1968).
48. When the simplifying assumption that everyone has the same level of wealth is made more realistic, the statement of this principle becomes more complicated. However, the basic idea that the fine should be high in order to save enforcement costs still applies.

that impose relatively small costs on others. Although there is nothing logically wrong with the preceding argument, it is premised on an assumption — risk neutrality — that is not likely to be correct when the fine is as large as the wealth of the individuals whose behavior is being controlled. Although individuals may care only about the expected loss if the worst possible loss is small relative to their wealth, they are likely to care as well about the actual probability and magnitude of the loss if the worst possible loss is large relative to their wealth. We will therefore reexamine the law enforcement problem when individuals are assumed to be risk averse.

The Risk-Averse Case

The residents of Econville can still be optimally deterred from double parking if they are risk averse. If detection is certain, a $10 fine would achieve this, as before, since their risk aversion is irrelevant. If detection is not certain, a risk-averse person would double-park only if the benefit from double parking exceeds the amount of money that the person would be willing to pay with certainty to avoid the risk of the fine. This amount of money is referred to as the *certainty equivalent* of the fine. For example, suppose the probability of detection is .1 and the fine is $100, as before, so the expected fine is $10. By definition, a risk-neutral person would be willing to pay only up to the expected fine to avoid it. Thus, as seen above, a risk-neutral person would double-park only if the benefit from double parking exceeds $10. But a risk-averse person would be willing to pay more than the expected fine to avoid it. Suppose, for example, that a risk-averse resident of Econville would be willing to pay as much as $11 with certainty to avoid the one-in-ten chance of having to pay a $100 fine. In other words, the certainty equivalent of the fine is $11. Then he would double-park only if his benefit from double parking exceeds $11. Since the cost imposed on others from double parking is only $10, there would be too few instances of double parking. *But this problem can be overcome by lowering the fine.* For example, given the probability of detection of .1, suppose the fine is $90, so the expected fine is $9. And suppose that a risk-averse resident of Econville would be willing to pay up to $10 — the certainty equivalent — to avoid this risk. Then he would double-park only if his benefit from doing so exceeded $10, the desired outcome.

The same result can be achieved when the probability of detection is .001. Suppose then that the fine would have to be as low as $2,000 to avoid overdeterring the residents of Econville. In other words, given their aversion to risk, they would be indifferent between paying $10 with certainty — the certainty equivalent — and facing the risk of a one-in-a-thousand chance of having to pay a $2,000 fine. Thus, even though the expected fine is only $2, they would double-park only if their benefits from doing so exceed $10.

Table 9 summarizes the discussion thus far of the double-parking example when individuals are risk averse. The first three columns of the table show, for each probability of detection, the fine that results in a certainty equivalent of $10, given the assumed risk aversion of the residents of Econville (ignore for now the remaining columns of the table). Table 9 and the preceding discussion illustrate an important general point regarding optimal deterrence when individuals are risk averse: Given the probability of detection, it is always possible to set the level of the fine so that the certainty equivalent of the fine — how much a person would be willing to pay with certainty to avoid the risk of being fined — equals the cost to others of that person's harmful activity.[49] The person then will engage in the harmful activity only when his benefits from doing so exceed the costs. Thus, it is always possible to achieve optimal deterrence, whether individuals are risk neutral or risk averse. The only difference is that, given the probability of detection, the optimal fine will have to be lower for a risk-averse person than

49. This statement is not correct if the probability of detection is very low. This is because, given a low enough probability, even a fine equal to the wealth of the individual being controlled will result in a certainty equivalent that is less than the cost to others of that individual's activity. (An analogous point would apply if individuals are risk neutral: Given a very low probability of detection, even a fine equal to an individual's wealth may result in an expected fine that is too low.) This problem does not arise in the double-parking example because of the particular values chosen for the lowest probability considered and for the wealth of Econville residents.

TABLE 9

Law Enforcement Example — Residents Risk Averse

Probability of Detection	Fine	Certainty Equivalent	Expected Fine	Per Person Risk-Bearing Costs	Total Risk-Bearing Costs	Total Enforcement Costs	Risk-Bearing Costs Plus Enforcement Costs
(1)	(2)	(3)	(4)[a]	(5)[b]	(6)[c]	(7)	(8)
1.0	$10	$10	$10	$0	$0	$500,000	$500,000
.1	$90	$10	$9	$1	$100,000	$50,000	$150,000
.001	$2,000	$10	$2	$8	$800,000	$500	$800,500

a. Equals column (1) times column (2).
b. Equals column (3) minus column (4).
c. Equals column (5) times 100,000.

79

for a risk-neutral person. Otherwise, the risk-averse person would be overdeterred.

It might appear at this point that the optimal system of law enforcement when individuals are risk averse is one in which, as when individuals are risk neutral, a low probability of detection is chosen in order to save enforcement costs. It is true in the example that optimal deterrence can be achieved with the least expenditure on enforcement by using the lowest probability of detection. But this is only half of the story. The lower the probability of detection and the higher the fine, the more risk that is imposed on those individuals who do double-park. Recall from the discussion in Chapter 7 that it is desirable to reduce or eliminate the risk borne by risk-averse persons. In the law enforcement context, this can be done by raising the probability of detection and lowering the fine accordingly. In the limit, if detection is certain, no risk is imposed on those individuals who double-park. Thus, there is a conflict between minimizing the cost of enforcement and minimizing the "cost" of bearing risk. The optimal probability of detection is the one that minimizes the *sum* of these costs. Before applying this principle to the double-parking example, we need to be more explicit about what is meant by the cost of bearing risk.

As seen in Chapter 7, the value of eliminating an unwanted risk can be measured by the difference between the expected value of the risk and the greatest amount of money the person bearing the risk would pay to avoid it.[50] In the example there, a person was willing to pay up to $45,000 with certainty to avoid a risk with an expected loss of $40,000. Thus, the value of removing the risk would be $5,000. Equivalently, instead of saying that the value of removing the risk would be $5,000, we can say that the cost of bearing the risk is $5,000. In general, using the terminology of certainty equivalence, the cost of bearing a risk is the difference between the certainty equivalent of the risk — how much one would be willing to pay to avoid it — and the expected value of the risk.

These observations can now be applied to the double-parking example. Refer again to Table 9. The first three columns

50. See p. 53 above.

show that, given the probability of detection, the fine is chosen so that the certainty equivalent of the fine is $10. This guarantees that only those individuals whose benefits from double parking exceed the costs will double-park. It was assumed earlier in this chapter that there are 100,000 such individuals in Econville each year. The fourth column in Table 9 computes the expected fine. The fifth column shows, for each person who double-parks, the cost of bearing the risk of the fine. For example, if the probability of detection is .1 and the fine is $90, the expected fine is $9. Since a resident of Econville would be willing to pay $10 — the certainty equivalent — to avoid this risk, his risk-bearing cost is $1. The sixth column shows the total risk-bearing costs for the 100,000 residents of Econville who double-park and who are therefore subject to the risk of being fined. The seventh column reproduces the enforcement cost data from Table 8, and the last column shows the sum of the risk-bearing costs and the enforcement costs.

It is clear from the last column of Table 9 that the optimal system of law enforcement in this example is to choose a probability of detection of .1 and a fine of $90. Although this choice does not minimize enforcement costs alone or risk-bearing costs alone, it does minimize their sum. Relative to this choice, using the .001 probability of detection is inefficient because it increases risk-bearing costs by $700,000 ($800,000 − $100,000), but reduces enforcement costs by only $49,500 ($50,000 − $500). And raising the probability so that detection is certain is inefficient because it increases enforcement costs by $450,000 ($500,000 − $50,000), while reducing risk-bearing costs by only $100,000.

The discussion of the double-parking example when the residents are assumed to be risk averse illustrates the following general observations: If individuals are risk averse, then the efficient system of law enforcement is one in which the fine generally is not as large as possible and the probability of detection generally is not as low as it would be if individuals were risk neutral. This is because the savings in enforcement costs from using a high fine and a low probability must be balanced against the increased risk imposed on those individuals for whom it is efficient to engage in the harmful activity. Thus, the optimal

probability of detection and fine depend on how much enforcement costs fall as the probability of detection decreases and on
how risk averse the relevant individuals are. Note that if these
individuals are neutral with respect to risk, then, according to
this argument, there is no reason not to raise the fine to the
wealth of the individuals being controlled in order to lower the
probability of detection. However, as mentioned earlier, it is not
plausible to assume that individuals are risk neutral when their
entire wealth is at risk.

An important assumption in the discussion of the double-
parking example was that it is efficient for some individuals to
engage in the harmful activity. This seems to be a reasonable
assumption in the context of double parking. But there are other
harmful activities in which the benefits from engaging in them
are never — or hardly ever — greater than the costs they impose
on others. For example, this would generally be the case with
respect to most activities classified as serious crimes, such as
assault and battery or drunken driving. For these types of activities, the optimal number of individuals engaging in them is, let
us suppose, zero. If deterrence is successful, no one will be
participating in the activity, and, therefore, no one will be bearing the risk created by the fine. Thus, the optimal system of law
enforcement would be one in which the fine is as high as possible and the probability is correspondingly low *even if* the individuals whose behavior is being controlled are risk averse. There
will not be any risk imposed on these individuals if deterrence is
successful.[51]

51. These observations can be illustrated in Table 9 with one modification. Instead of assuming that the efficient number of double-parking
violations is 100,000, assume that this number is zero. Column (5) still can be
interpreted as the risk-bearing cost for each individual who engages in the
harmful activity. But column (6), total risk-bearing costs (which equals column (5) multiplied by the efficient number of double-parking violators),
would now consist of entries of zero. Thus, column (8), total risk-bearing
costs plus total enforcement costs, would be the same as column (7), total
enforcement costs. The optimal system of enforcement would then be to
deter double parking by a probability of detection of .001 and a fine of $10,000,
even though the residents of Econville are risk averse.

Obviously, in practice there are individuals who do engage in these kinds of harmful activities. But the general point of this discussion is valid nonetheless. The smaller the number of individuals whose benefits from engaging in a harmful activity exceed the costs imposed on others, the lower the optimal probability of detection and the higher the optimal fine. Although there will be risk imposed on those individuals who do engage in the activity, the aggregate risk-bearing costs will be relatively small since there are few such individuals. It is therefore desirable to use a relatively low probability of detection and a relatively high fine in order to save enforcement costs.

Another important assumption that was implicit in the discussion of the double-parking example was that there were no mistakes in the law enforcement system. In general, if individuals are risk averse, then to the extent that there are mistakes, the optimal probability of detection should be higher and the optimal fine should be lower than they otherwise would be. To see why, consider the control of speeding rather than double parking, and suppose police radar equipment occasionally malfunctions and indicates that someone is speeding when in fact he is not. Then the risk created by the probability of detection and the fine is imposed on *all* drivers, not just those who speed. Hence, if mistakes are possible, the risk-bearing costs would be larger than otherwise, and the optimal system of law enforcement generally would involve a higher probability of detection and a lower fine in order to reduce these costs.

This chapter has provided an overview of the economic analysis of law enforcement. A central idea in this analysis, associated with the work of Gary Becker, is that enforcement costs can be reduced, without sacrificing optimal deterrence, by lowering the probability of detection and raising the fine accordingly. We have seen that enforcement cost considerations are of primary importance if individuals are neutral with respect to risk. These considerations are also of principal importance if individuals are averse to risk, *provided* that optimal deterrence leads to no one engaging in the harmful activity and that there are no mistakes in the enforcement system. However, if individuals are risk averse and if it is optimal for some of them to engage in the activity, or if there are mistakes, then risk-bearing considerations also are relevant. We have seen that taking these considerations into account generally increases the optimal probability of detection and decreases the optimal fine. The particular probability and fine combination that is optimal depends on the tradeoff between enforcement costs and risk-bearing costs.

CHAPTER 11

COMPETITIVE MARKETS

In the nuisance law and breach of contract applications, it was assumed that at least one of the parties to the dispute was a firm rather than an individual. Other kinds of disputes in which firms are frequently involved include, for example, those related to widespread pollution or defective products. These are the next two applications that will be discussed. Before addressing them, it will be useful to describe certain features of competitive markets.

A *competitive market* is a market in which there are many firms producing the same commodity and many consumers purchasing it. In such a market, each producer believes he has no control over the prevailing price of the commodity because he supplies such a small fraction of it. Similarly, each consumer believes he has no control over the price since he buys such a small fraction of the total amount sold.[52] Our discussion of competitive markets will assume that firms presently in the industry are free to leave the industry if profit opportunities are better elsewhere and that potential firms are free to enter this industry if it is more profitable than alternative investment opportunities. This assumption of free exit and free entry of

52. More generally, one could characterize markets in terms of the degree to which each seller or buyer has control over the market price. A competitive market is one important special case. A monopolistic market, in which there is a single seller who sets the price and many buyers, is another. Although the next two applications — pollution control and products liability — could be considered in the context of markets that are not competitive, it is beyond the scope of this book to undertake this task. The style of analysis would be similar to that used in the competitive case (although the specific conclusions would differ).

firms defines what economists refer to as the *long run*.[53] When all firms that want to leave the industry have done so and all firms that want to enter have done so, the industry is said to be in *long-run equilibrium*.

Price Equals Cost

A basic principle of competitive markets in long-run equilibrium is that the price of the product will equal its cost of production.[54] Why this must be so can be easily explained by an example. Suppose it costs $100 to manufacture a lawnmower. If the price of lawnmowers were below $100, say $75, then a producer would lose $25 for every lawnmower produced. It would be more profitable for the firm to go out of business — that is, to exit — and to earn nothing than to lose money producing lawnmowers. Thus, in equilibrium — after all firms that want to exit have done so — the price of lawnmowers would not be less than $100 if they are being produced. If the price of lawnmowers were above $100, say $150, then lawnmower production would be very profitable. New firms would enter this industry because of its profitability. As a result, the supply of lawnmowers would increase, a glut would occur, and the price would begin to fall. As long as the price exceeds the cost of production, firms would continue to enter this industry and the price would continue to fall. Thus, in equilibrium, the price of lawnmowers would not exceed $100. This discussion shows that, because firms are free to exit and to enter the industry, the price of the product will equal its cost of production.

If the price of a product equals its cost of production, a firm producing it will just break even. This does not mean, however, that the managers of the firm will not receive any compensation or that the owners of the firm will not earn any return on their

53. In the *short run*, it is assumed that existing firms can exit but no new firms can enter.

54. Readers who have previously studied economics will recall that in a competitive long-run equilibrium, a firm's average cost equals its marginal cost. Thus, there is no ambiguity in the text in referring simply to the "cost of production."

investment in the firm. The managers' compensation and the owners' returns are already included as part of the cost of production.

The Efficiency of Competitive Pricing

Whether the fact that the competitive price equals production costs is desirable is answered by another basic principle of competitive markets. This principle states that if "all relevant costs" are taken into account, a competitive market will lead to the efficient outcome. What is meant by "all relevant costs" will become clear in the next two applications; for now, just interpret this as referring to the cost of production.

To understand why the second principle is true, consider the lawnmower example again. People value lawnmowers differently. For example, someone with a large yard would be willing to pay more for a lawnmower than someone with a small yard. Assume, as before, that lawnmowers cost $100 to produce. Suppose, however, that lawnmowers sell for $150. Then someone who values a lawnmower at $125 will not buy one. But this is inefficient because the benefit of the lawnmower, $125, exceeds its production cost, $100. There would be an efficiency gain of $25 if this person were to get a lawnmower. Alternatively, suppose that lawnmowers are priced at $75. Then someone who values a lawnmower at $85 will purchase one. But this is inefficient, too, because the benefit of the lawnmower is less than its production cost of $100. There will be an efficiency loss of $15 when this person buys a lawnmower.

In general, if a good is priced above its cost of production, then some individuals who value the good more than its cost will not buy it, which is an inefficient outcome; and if a good is priced below its production cost, then some individuals who value it less than its cost will buy it nonetheless, which is also an inefficient outcome. Only if the price of the good equals its cost of production will those people who value it more than its cost buy it and those who value it less not buy it. This is required to achieve an efficient outcome. Since, according to the first basic principle, the price of a good in a competitive market equals its cost of production, a competitive market will lead to an efficient outcome.

We will now consider two final applications — pollution control and products liability — that make use of these observations about competitive markets.

CHAPTER 12

SEVENTH APPLICATION — POLLUTION CONTROL

In this chapter we will investigate the efficiency of different legal rules for controlling pollution when the polluters are firms in a competitive industry in long-run equilibrium. The discussion will be based on an example in which firms emitting air pollution harm households downwind of the pollution. For simplicity, it is assumed that the victims of the pollution are not also consumers of the product manufactured by the firms. In the example, the harm to the victims depends on whether the polluters filter their smoke before discharging it into the atmosphere. The filtering process reduces the level of pollution but does not eliminate it entirely. It also increases the polluters' cost of production. The victims of the pollution are assumed to be unable to affect the damage they suffer. (This assumption will be reconsidered below.) The data for this example are described in Table 10 for a representative firm (ignore for now the last three columns). Note that, once the filtering decision has been made, there is no uncertainty with respect to the harm; thus, the issue of risk allocation does not arise in this example.

Given the data in Table 10, it is clear that the efficient solution involves filtering the pollution before discharging it. Although filtering increases production costs by $15 for each unit of the firm's output, it reduces pollution damages by $30 for each unit produced. Another way to express this is to note that the *full cost* of the product — the firm's production cost plus the victims' pollution damage — is $140 if filtering does not occur but only $125 if it does occur. This is shown in the third column of Table 10.

TABLE 10

Pollution Control Example

Behavior of Firm	Firm's Production Cost Per Unit	Victim's Pollution Damage Per Unit	Full Cost Per Unit	Firm's Cost Per Unit under Negligence	Firm's Cost Per Unit under Strict Liability
	(1)	(2)	(3)	(4)	(5)
Don't filter	$100	$40	$140	$140	$140
Filter	$115	$10	$125	$115	$125

There is a second aspect of the efficient solution in this problem. Even if filtering occurs for each unit of the good produced, an inefficient amount of the good may be produced. Equivalently, since goods are produced to satisfy the demands of consumers, an inefficient amount of the good may be consumed. For reasons seen in the previous chapter, an inefficient amount will be consumed either if some individuals buy the good who value it less than its full cost or if some individuals do not buy the good who value it more than its full cost. Thus, since the full cost of the good is $125 — assuming that filtering occurs — only individuals who value the good at $125 or more per unit should consume it.

Only Polluters Determine Harm

We will now examine whether the liability rules of negligence and strict liability lead to the efficient control of pollution. Under negligence, suppose firms are liable only if they do not filter. Then, as shown in the fourth column in Table 10, a firm's cost, including its liability payments, would be $140 if it does not filter and $115 if it does. Clearly, each firm will choose to filter. Thus, in long-run equilibrium, the price will be $115 per unit. If the price were higher, entry would occur due to the profit opportunities, and if the price were lower, firms would leave the industry since they would be losing money. But if the equilibrium price is $115, excessive consumption of the good will occur. Given that firms filter, the full cost is $125, including the $10 residual pollution damage borne by victims (see Table 10). Thus, at a price of $115, there will be persons who value the good at less than its full cost — for example, at $120 — but who will buy it nonetheless.

This example illustrates a general point about the effects of negligence rules in competitive markets: Even though the rule of negligence can, with an appropriate standard of care, induce firms to take an efficient amount of care, it generally leads to an inefficient level of output because the market price does not completely reflect the full cost of the product. Specifically, the price does not reflect the residual damages that occur even when each firm is taking an efficient amount of care. Consequently, too much of the good will be consumed.[55]

Now consider the rule of strict liability, under which firms will be made liable for the victims' pollution damages whether they filter or not. Then, as shown in the last column of Table 10, each firm's cost, including liability payments, would be $140 if it does not filter and $125 if it does. Each firm will therefore choose to filter. Thus, in long-run equilibrium, the price of the good will be $125, and, since the full cost is also $125, the amount of the good bought by consumers will be efficient.

This example illustrates a general observation about strict liability in competitive markets: Strict liability can induce firms to take an efficient amount of care and can induce consumers to purchase an efficient amount of the good. The latter effect occurs because the market price reflects the full cost of the product, including the damages that remain even when each firm is taking an efficient amount of care.

Victims Also Affect Harm

In many pollution situations, the victims of the pollution also can affect their damages from pollution. For example, they

---

55. This problem would not arise if, by taking the efficient amount of care, *all* pollution is eliminated. In general, however, some residual damage will occur.

might be able to paint their homes with more expensive pollution-resistant paint or move to a less polluted neighborhood. The conclusions in this chapter regarding the rules of negligence and strict liability would have to be modified somewhat if both the polluters' behavior and the victims' behavior can affect the level of damages. Since the analysis of this problem closely parallels the corresponding analysis of automobile accidents in Chapter 6 (when both the driver and the pedestrian can affect the pedestrian's expected accident costs),[56] the discussion here will be brief.

Suppose for concreteness that the efficient solution now requires not only that the polluters filter but also that the victims paint their homes with special paint. This paint reduces the victims' damages, but it does not eliminate the damages. The efficient solution still requires that only those consumers who value the good more than its full cost purchase it. Note, however, that the appropriate full cost now equals the polluters' cost of production plus the residual damages that occur both when the polluter is filtering *and* when the victims are using the special paint.

Under the rule of negligence, a polluter will choose to filter in order to avoid the liability costs that he would otherwise incur. Given this decision, the victims will bear their own losses and will therefore have an appropriate incentive to use the pollution-resistant paint. Thus, as in the automobile accident example, the negligence rule can induce both the injurer and the victim to take appropriate care. However, the negligence rule will still fail to induce efficient decisions by consumers since the price of the good will not reflect the damages that occur even when the polluters and the victims are taking appropriate care.

Under strict liability, polluters will also choose to filter, as before. However, pollution victims will not have any incentive to use pollution-resistant paint since they will be fully compensated for their damages. Thus, for reasons described in Chapter 6 in the context of the automobile accident example, it is necessary to add a defense of contributory negligence in order to induce the pollution victims to take appropriate care. With this

56. See pp. 40-44 above.

defense, the rule of strict liability will be efficient with respect to both parties' care. Since the victims will choose not to be contributorily negligent, the polluters will be liable for the victims' residual damages. Thus, the price of the product will reflect these damages and an efficient amount will be purchased.

This discussion shows that the basic conclusions about strict liability and negligence in the pollution control example are not affected if the victims can reduce their damages by taking precautions. The basic problem under the negligence rule is that the price of the good produced by the polluters does not reflect the damages that still occur after all of the parties have taken appropriate care. This problem is overcome under the strict liability rule because the polluter is made liable for these residual damages. However, if the victims can affect the level of damages, it is necessary to add a defense of contributory negligence to the strict liability rule in order to create incentives for them to take appropriate precautions.

The conclusions in this chapter are similar to those derived in Chapter 6 in the context of automobile accidents. This should not be surprising since the basic problems that liability rules have to solve in the two contexts are also similar. In both chapters, the rules of strict liability with a defense of contributory negligence and negligence were found to be equally effective in controlling the injurer's care (the polluter's filtering decision here, the driver's speed in Chapter 6) as well as the victim's care (the homeowner's painting decision here, the pedestrian's decision whether to walk or to run in Chapter 6). And, in both chapters, strict liability was found to be superior to negligence in controlling the injurer's activity level — which corresponds to the output of the industry here, the amount of driving in Chapter 6.[57] The main difference between the two chapters is that there was no activity-level issue with respect to the victim in the pollution control context. This is why strict liability with a

57. This statement presumes that the standard of care under the negligence rule is not defined in terms of the injurer's activity level for the reasons discussed in Chapter 6. See pp. 46-47 above.

defense of contributory negligence was found to be efficient here but was found to induce excessive participation in the activity by the pedestrian in Chapter 6. In practice, however, there might well be an activity-level issue with respect to pollution victims, too. For example, suppose a victim's damage depends not only on whether he uses pollution-resistant paint but also on the size of the house he buys. The conclusions in this chapter then would exactly parallel those in Chapter 6.

CHAPTER 13

EIGHTH APPLICATION —
PRODUCTS LIABILITY

We will now use several of the principles developed in the chapters on competitive markets and on risk bearing and insurance to evaluate the efficiency of alternative liability rules for dealing with product accidents. The analysis will be based on an example in which a soda manufacturer must decide whether to use bottles or cans. Bottles are cheaper to produce but have higher expected accident losses.[58] It will be assumed that the victim of the accident is the purchaser of the good and that, for simplicity, the victim cannot affect expected accident losses by taking care. (The possibilities that the victim is a "third party" — such as a bystander — and that the victim can reduce expected losses by taking care will be considered briefly at the end of this chapter.) The data for the example are provided in Table 11.

Given these data, it is clear that the efficient solution involves selling soda in cans rather than in bottles. Although using cans increases production costs by 3 cents per unit, it lowers expected accident losses by 8 cents. Equivalently, the full cost of the product — the firm's production cost plus the consumer's expected accident loss — is less with cans (45 cents) than with bottles (50 cents). Another aspect of the efficient solution involves the purchasers' consumption decisions. Assuming cans are used, the full cost of soda is 45 cents; therefore, only individuals who value soda at 45 cents or more should drink it. Since we are dealing with an accident situation, the efficient solution

58. These losses are assumed to have a monetary value. But see note 23 above.

TABLE 11

Products Liability Example

Behavior of Firm	Firm's Cost of Production Per Unit	Probability of Accident to Consumer	Loss if Accident	Expected Accident Loss	Full Cost Per Unit
	(1)	(2)	(3)	(4)	(5)
Use bottle	40 cents	1/100,000	$10,000	10 cents	50 cents
Use can	43 cents	1/200,000	$4,000	2 cents	45 cents

also will be concerned with the allocation of risk. Initially, however, this consideration will be put aside by assuming that producers and consumers are risk neutral.

Consumers Have Perfect Information

It will be useful to provide a benchmark by first comparing product liability rules when consumers are assumed to have perfect information about expected accident losses. We will consider the rules of strict liability, negligence, and no liability. Under strict liability, firms are liable to consumers for their losses whenever an accident occurs. Then, given the data in Table 11, each firm's cost per unit, including expected liability payments, would be 50 cents if bottles are used and 45 cents if cans are used. Thus, in long-run equilibrium, the price per bottle would be 50 cents and the price per can would be 45 cents. Consumers clearly will prefer to purchase soda in cans.[59] Moreover, given the price of soda in cans, they will purchase an efficient number of cans since the price reflects the full cost of the product. Strict liability is therefore efficient both with re- spect to the "care" exercised by each firm — whether, in the example, cans or bottles are used — and with respect to the output of the industry.

59. Consumers are assumed to enjoy drinking soda just as much out of a can as out of a bottle.

Under negligence, suppose firms are liable only if they produce soda in bottles. Then, referring to Table 11, a firm's cost, and therefore the price, would be 50 cents if bottles are used and 43 cents if cans are used. Because consumers are assumed to have correct information about expected accident losses, they will in effect add 2 cents to the price of cans since they bear their own losses when cans are used. Consumers still obviously will prefer cans to bottles. Although soda in cans will sell for 43 cents, consumers will buy the correct number since the *effective* price, including the additional 2 cents in expected accident costs, is 45 cents. Thus, negligence also is efficient both with respect to care and to output.

Under no liability, consumers bear their own losses regardless of firms' behavior. Thus, a firm's cost, and the price, would be 40 cents if bottles are used and 43 cents if cans are used. Since consumers will in effect add 10 cents to the price of bottles but only 2 cents to the price of cans, consumers will be interested only in buying soda in cans. And since they will treat the effective price of soda in cans as 45 cents, they will purchase the correct number. Thus, no liability also is efficient with respect to care and output.

This discussion illustrates a general result in the economic analysis of product liability rules: When producers and consumers are risk neutral and consumers have perfect information about product risks, the choice of liability rule is irrelevant. Every rule will lead to the efficient outcome both in terms of the care exercised by producers and the output of the industry.[60]

Consumers Underestimate Product Risks

It is unrealistic in many product markets to assume that consumers have perfect information about expected accident losses. This assumption seems especially inappropriate for

60. This result can be viewed as an application of the simple version of the Coase Theorem: If there are zero transaction costs, the efficient outcome will occur regardless of the choice of legal rule. See p. 12 above. The assumption that consumers have perfect information is analogous to the assumption of zero transaction costs.

products that cause harm very infrequently. We will therefore examine the effects of imperfect consumer information on the optimal choice of a product liability rule. To see these effects in the simplest way possible, it will be assumed that consumers completely underestimate the risks — that is, that they think the product is perfectly safe.

The earlier discussion of strict liability is not affected by imperfect consumer information about product risks. Because producers are liable, they would still be willing to offer bottles at a price of 50 cents or cans at a price of 45 cents. Consumers will still purchase only cans and will, given the price, buy the correct number. The efficiency of strict liability does not depend on the information of consumers for the following reason. Because consumers know they will be fully compensated for product accident losses, they will treat the good as if it were perfectly safe, *regardless of their information about the product risks*. But, because firms are liable for the actual losses, consumers will be forced to take the true risks into account through the prices charged by firms.

Under negligence, firms would be willing, as before, to sell soda in bottles for 50 cents, given that they will be liable for the losses that occur, or in cans for 43 cents, given that they will not be liable. Now, however, consumers will not add 2 cents to the price of cans to account for expected accident losses (since they are assumed to be ignorant of the product risks). They will therefore still purchase soda in cans since soda is less expensive in cans than in bottles. However, too much soda will be purchased because the price does not reflect the expected accident losses. For example, someone who values soda at .44 cents will buy a can for 43 cents even though the full cost is 45 cents. The important point about negligence when consumers underestimate product risks is that, while producers can still be induced to take appropriate care, consumers will buy too much of the good because they will not fully take into account the accident losses that remain.

Under no liability, firms would be willing, as before, to offer bottles at a price of 40 cents or cans at a price of 43 cents. Now, however, consumers will not add 10 cents to the price of bottles or 2 cents to the price of cans to reflect expected accident losses. As a result, consumers will purchase soda in bottles and, because they do not take account of expected accident losses, will buy too much soda. Thus, when consumers underestimate expected accident losses, the rule of no liability leads both to too little care and to too much output.

The discussion thus far illustrates the following proposition: When consumers underestimate product risks, only the rule of strict liability is efficient both with respect to the care exercised by firms and the purchase decisions of consumers. The rule of negligence can induce producers to take appropriate care, but consumers will purchase too much of the good. And the rule of no liability is deficient both with respect to care and with respect to output. Thus, strict liability is, in effect, a substitute for perfect consumer information.[61]

Risk Aversion

It has been assumed thus far that both producers and consumers are risk neutral. This may be a reasonable assumption for some product liability problems, such as those in which the product defect leads to the destruction of the product itself but does not cause additional damage to persons or property. In other situations, however, the assumption of risk neutrality would be unrealistic, especially if there is substantial additional damage. This would be the case, for example, with respect to exploding soda bottles or the hazards related to cans.

We therefore will reconsider product liability rules assuming that producers and/or consumers may be risk averse. Under strict liability, product risks are borne entirely by the producers, whereas under negligence, the losses are left entirely on consumers (assuming that producers meet the standard of care). Under no liability, the risks are obviously also borne entirely by consumers. Since negligence is equivalent to no liability in terms of risk allocation, but is preferred to no liability in terms of inducing producers to take care, the rule of no liability will not be considered further.

61. If consumers *over*estimated product risks, then producers would have an incentive to voluntarily provide full product warranties. These warranties would lead to the same outcome as a rule of strict liability.

Once risk aversion is taken into account, the availability of insurance is, of course, an important consideration. Since the analysis of the interaction between product liability rules and insurance closely parallels the corresponding analysis in Chapter 9 in the context of automobile accidents,[62] the discussion here will be relatively brief and will deal exclusively with risk allocation issues. (The reader should keep in mind, however, that the choice of a product liability rule will also affect the care exercised by the parties and the output of the industry.)

If insurance is not available to either party, then, with respect to the allocation of risk, strict liability is ideal if consumers are risk averse and producers are risk neutral, whereas negligence is ideal if the reverse is true. If both producers and consumers are risk averse, then a modified version of strict liability should be used, with the level of liability depending on the relative risk aversion of producers and consumers. The more risk averse consumers are relative to producers, the higher the level of liability should be.

If ideal liability insurance and first-party accident insurance policies are available, then both strict liability and negligence are efficient in terms of risk allocation. Under strict liability, producers will be fully insured by liability insurance, and under negligence, consumers will be fully insured by first-party accident insurance.

Finally, suppose that insurance policies provide less than complete coverage because of the problem of moral hazard. Under strict liability, producers would bear some risk because, given the moral hazard problem with respect to their care, liability insurance policies would be incomplete. Under negligence, consumers would also bear some risk because, for reasons to be explained, there is a moral hazard problem with respect to their behavior and first-party accident insurance policies would therefore be incomplete.

Although it has been assumed that consumers cannot affect their expected accident losses by taking care, they generally *can* reduce their expected accident losses by purchasing fewer units of the good. Thus, to avoid a moral hazard problem with respect

---

62. See pp. 65-71 above.

to their consumption decision, the premium for first-party accident insurance would have to be based on the amount purchased. For example, since the expected accident loss from drinking soda in cans rises proportionally with the number of cans purchased, the insurance premium would also have to rise proportionally with the quantity purchased. If the premium paid does not depend on the number of cans purchased, then consumers will buy too much soda. In general, it is obviously difficult, if not impossible, for insurance companies to monitor consumers' purchases. This would certainly be the case, for example, with respect to soda consumption. Consequently, first-party accident insurance policies would provide less than full coverage in order to discourage consumers from purchasing an excessive amount of the good.

Given both imperfect liability insurance and imperfect first-party accident insurance, the optimal choice between strict liability and negligence in terms of risk allocation depends on the relative risk aversion of producers and consumers. Under strict liability, producers will bear some risk because of incomplete liability insurance coverage, but consumers will be insured by the liability payment. Under negligence, producers will be free of liability (assuming they meet the standard of care), but consumers will bear some risk because of incomplete first-party accident insurance coverage. Thus, to the extent that consumers are more risk averse than producers, strict liability would be preferred to negligence, and vice versa.

The moral hazard problem with respect to the consumer's purchase decision may not arise in some circumstances. For many consumer products — such as washing machines, lawnmowers, and toaster ovens — it is reasonable to assume that each consumer needs only one unit of the good. Thus, still assuming that the consumer cannot affect his expected accident losses by taking care, there would not be any kind of moral hazard problem with respect to these goods. Consequently, first-party accident insurance policies would provide full coverage. Negligence would then be superior to strict liability in terms of risk allocation. Under strict liability, producers would still bear some risk because of incomplete liability insurance coverage, but under negligence, neither producers nor consumers would now bear any risk.

Consumers Can Take Care

An important simplifying assumption in the discussion thus far has been that the consumer cannot affect his expected accident losses by taking care. This assumption is obviously not realistic in some product liability situations. For example, the probability that a soda bottle or can will cause harm certainly depends on how it is handled by the purchaser. If the consumer can affect the expected losses by taking care, then the efficient solution to the accident problem also will involve his taking some appropriate level of care. Although the analysis of this issue is similar to the analysis of the pedestrian's care decision in the automobile accident example in Chapter 6,[63] there are some important differences because of the possibility considered here that the victim misperceives expected accident losses.

Under strict liability, a defense of contributory negligence would be required to get the consumer to take appropriate precautions. Assuming the consumer meets the standard of care, the producer will be liable for the consumer's losses and the earlier discussion of strict liability will be applicable. However, if the consumer underestimates the probability or magnitude of the harm, he will underestimate the value of meeting the standard of care applicable to him. If, as a result, he does not meet the standard, he would then bear his own losses. Consequently, the producer would not have an incentive to take care. Moreover, because the consumer underestimates his expected losses, he might not be willing to buy first-party accident insurance even if the premium equals his expected losses.

Under a negligence rule, the producer will take appropriate care in order to avoid liability, so the losses will be borne by the consumer. If the consumer underestimates the expected losses, he generally will not take the desired level of precautions and may not purchase first-party accident insurance. Thus, when consumers can affect expected accident losses by taking care but underestimate these losses, neither strict liability with a defense of contributory negligence nor negligence may be ideal with respect to the care exercised by the parties or with respect to the allocation of risk.

63. See pp. 40-44 above.

The discussion in this chapter has been premised on the assumption that the victim of the product accident is the purchaser of the product. In some product accident situations, the victim may be a *third party*. For example, a defective lawnmower may throw a rock that hits a bystander rather than the lawnmower owner. When the victim is a third party, the argument for using a strict liability rule is strengthened relative to the argument for using a negligence rule. The reason is straightforward. Under strict liability, the price of the product will equal its full cost, including the expected accident losses *to third parties*. Consumers will therefore purchase the correct amount. Under negligence, the price will not reflect the expected accident losses to third parties because producers will choose not to be negligent. And since consumers do not suffer the harm, they will ignore these losses when deciding how much of the good to purchase. Consequently, they will buy too much. This problem is not different in kind from the one that occurred when the victim was a consumer. But then, at least to the extent that the consumer perceived the magnitude of the expected losses, he would effectively add that amount to the price of the good. Thus, the problem with the negligence rule, that it encourages too much output, is generally worse when the victim is a third party.

It should be clear by now that the preferred liability rule for dealing with product accidents depends on several, possibly conflicting, considerations. If the victims of the accidents are consumers of the product and if they have perfect information about the product risks, then both the rule of strict liability with a defense of contributory negligence and the rule of negligence can induce both producers and consumers to take appropriate care and can induce consumers to purchase the correct output. However, if consumers underestimate the expected accident losses, then only strict liability with a defense of contributory negligence will achieve these results, *provided* that consumers meet the standard of care applicable to them. Because of their imperfect information, they might not perceive the value of meeting this standard. If, as a result, they do not meet it, then even strict liability with a defense of contributory negligence will be inefficient. (If the victims of the product accidents are third parties rather than consumers, the case for strict liability is strengthened relative to the case for negligence.)

Once considerations of risk allocation are added to the above discussion, matters become even more complicated (unless ideal insurance is available). If insurance is not available, or if only imperfect insurance is available because of the problem of moral hazard, then, generally speaking, strict liability becomes more desirable relative to negligence to the extent that the victims are more risk averse than the producers, and vice versa. When all of the effects of product liability rules are taken into account — the effects on the producers' care, on the victims' care, on industry output, and on risk allocation — it is clear that, in general, no one rule will be best in every respect. What rule should be used depends on the relative importance of these competing considerations in each particular type of products liability situation.

CHAPTER 14

EFFICIENCY AND EQUITY RECONSIDERED

The discussion of efficiency and equity in Chapter 2 showed that there is no conflict between these goals if income can be costlessly redistributed. In essence, this is because any inequity in the distribution of income caused by the pursuit of efficiency could be corrected at no cost. The assumption that redistribution is costless was made at the end of that chapter. We will now reconsider this assumption, first with respect to the redistribution of income by means of the government's tax and transfer system and then with respect to redistribution by legal rules.

Redistribution by Taxes and Transfers

In general, the redistribution of income by taxes or transfers is costly in the following sense. Recall from the discussion in Chapter 11 that when the price of a good equals its cost of production, only those individuals who value the good more than its cost will purchase it. This was seen to be efficient. The good used to illustrate this point in Chapter 11 was a lawnmower that cost $100 to produce. Suppose that rich people are more likely to purchase lawnmowers than poor people because they are more likely to live in houses than in apartment buildings. Then, by imposing an excise tax on purchasers of lawnmowers, the government would raise more tax revenue from the rich than from the poor. Assuming that the revenue is spent in a way that does not disproportionately favor the rich — say it benefits everyone equally — then the net effect of the tax would be to redistribute income from the rich to the poor. However, an inevitable byproduct of this redistribution is that the price of lawnmowers will be "distorted" — that is, the effective price of lawnmowers, including the tax, will exceed their cost of production. As a consequence, too few lawnmowers will be bought. For example, if the excise tax is $10 per lawnmower, then everyone who values lawnmowers more than the production cost of $100 but less than $110 will not purchase one, an inefficient outcome. In general, to redistribute income by an excise tax it is necessary to sacrifice some efficiency with respect to consumption decisions. This loss of efficiency is a cost of redistributing income.[64]

The same kind of problem applies to income taxes, although not in as obvious a way. To see the distortion from income taxes, first note that leisure is a commodity desired by consumers just like any other commodity. The "price" of an hour of leisure is the income forgone from not working that hour. For example, suppose the wage rate in the widget industry is $25 per hour and that widget workers have some flexibility with regard to the number of hours they work. If widget workers did not have to pay income taxes, then they would sacrifice $25 to consume an hour of leisure. Thus, those individuals who valued another hour of leisure more than $25 would "buy" more leisure by working an hour less. But suppose widget workers faced a 20 percent income tax. Then for every hour worked, they would pay $5 to the government and retain $20. The "price" of leisure would therefore fall to $20 per hour. Now individuals who value leisure more than $20 per hour will work less.[65] Assuming that the $25 per hour wage reflects a worker's contribution to the value of the widgets produced, the income tax

64. There are also, of course, administrative costs incurred in implementing any tax (or transfer) system.

65. Actually, this statement might not be correct. To see why, suppose an individual's preferences are such that he wants to consume a particular set of goods and services before consuming any leisure. Then the imposition of an income tax will *increase* the number of hours he has to work in order to be able to purchase these goods and services. However, whether the tax leads individuals to increase or decrease the number of hours they work does not affect the general point that this example will be used to illustrate.

will cause an inefficient consumption decision regarding leisure. For example, a worker who values leisure at $21 per hour will work less even though the value of the worker's time in terms of widget production is $25 per hour. As in the case of the excise tax, the income tax distorts the price of some commodity — in this case leisure — and causes inefficient consumption decisions. Thus, it, too, imposes a cost in order to redistribute income.

Redistributing income by transfers rather than by taxes does not avoid the problem of distorting consumption decisions. For example, suppose the government subsidizes the price of electricity for low-income individuals. Then the individuals who receive the subsidy will face an effective price of electricity that is below the cost of producing electricity and they will therefore buy too much of it relative to what is efficient.[66] In general, any kind of tax or transfer used to redistribute income will distort the price of some commodity and will therefore have this kind of efficiency cost.

Can Legal Rules Redistribute Income?

Given the cost of redistributing income by taxes and transfers, the question naturally arises whether the legal system should be used to redistribute income. That legal rules *can* be used to redistribute income was suggested by the discussion in Chapter 3 of the distributional aspects of the Coase Theorem.[67] In the example in that chapter of the factory polluting the residents, recall, for example, that when there were no transaction costs, the choice between the right to pollute and the right to clean air redistributed income by the $150 cost of the smokescreen — the least-cost solution to the conflict. It does not follow from that discussion, however, that legal rules always affect the distribution of income. To understand why, it is useful

66. This statement obviously presumes that electricity would otherwise be priced according to its cost. In practice, however, electricity may not be priced this way by the public utilities providing it.

67. See pp. 12 & 13 above.

to distinguish between legal disputes in which the parties are in some kind of contractual relationship, including a market relationship, and disputes in which the parties are, in effect, "strangers" prior to the dispute. The breach of contract and products liability examples would be characterized as *contractual disputes*, while the nuisance law, automobile accident, and pollution control examples would be described as *disputes between strangers*.[68] (The products liability example is of the first type because the victim is a consumer; it would be of the second type if the victim were a third party.) It will be shown below that legal rules often cannot redistribute income in contractual disputes, whereas legal rules always can redistribute income in disputes between strangers.

To see why it is frequently difficult, if not impossible, to use legal rules to redistribute income in contractual disputes, consider again the discussion in Chapter 5 of breach of contract. In the example used there, a seller of widgets might want to breach the contract with an initial buyer if an offer from a third party materialized. Suppose it is desirable for equity reasons to redistribute income from the seller to the buyer. Giving the buyer the remedy of expectation damages makes the buyer as well off if the contract is breached as he would have been had it been performed. Giving the buyer the remedy of reliance damages or restitution damages makes the buyer worse off if the contract is breached. However, because the contract price the buyer and seller negotiate depends on what the remedy is, it does not follow from this discussion that the buyer is better off with the expectation remedy. Clearly, the seller will demand a higher price and the buyer will be willing to pay more if the buyer receives a larger payment in the event of a breach. Thus, considering both the higher initial contract price and the higher compensation in the event of a breach, the buyer may not be any better off with the expectation remedy. In general, the parties will take any distributional effects of breach of contract remedies into account when setting the contract price; thus, how

68. Because the law enforcement example was not characterized as a dispute between private parties, it will not be considered in the present discussion.

the joint benefits of entering into the contract are shared between the parties depends primarily, if not exclusively, on their relative bargaining strengths, not on the remedies available to them.

An analogous observation can be made about the products liability application when the victim of the product accident is a consumer of the good. Suppose, for example, it is desirable for equity reasons to redistribute income from producers to consumers. It was seen in Chapter 13 that under the rule of negligence, the producer will meet the standard of care, so consumers will bear their own losses. But under the rule of strict liability, consumers will be fully compensated for their losses (assuming, if there is a defense of contributory negligence, they meet the standard of care applicable to them). Consumers will not, however, be better off as a class under strict liability because the competitive long-run equilibrium price will rise by an amount equal to the producers' expected liability.[69] In general, then, whenever the parties to a dispute are in some kind of contractual or market relationship, it may be difficult, if not impossible, to use the legal system to redistribute income.

To see why legal rules can be used to redistribute income in disputes between strangers, consider again the discussion of automobile accidents in Chapter 6. In the simple version of the example employed there, a pedestrian's expected accident losses depended solely on whether a driver chose to drive slowly, moderately, or rapidly. Under a negligence rule, the pedestrian will bear his own losses because the driver will choose to meet the standard of care — to drive moderately — whereas under a strict liability rule the driver will have to compensate the pedestrian for his losses. Since there is no contractual or market relationship between the parties, there is no contract price or market price that can be adjusted when legal rules change. Thus, shifting from one liability rule to the other will redistribute income by the amount of the expected losses. (If, as discussed in

69. However, if the market for the product is not competitive, then consumers *may* be better off as a class under strict liability than under negligence. Since it is beyond the scope of this book to consider markets that are not competitive (see note 52 above), this point will not be considered further.

Chapter 9, the parties are risk averse and the driver can buy liability insurance and the pedestrian can buy first-party accident insurance, the redistribution will take the form of allocating the insurance premium to one party or the other rather than the risk of bearing the pedestrian's losses.)

Analogous observations can be made with respect to the nuisance law and pollution control applications. In the nuisance example discussed in Chapter 4 of a polluting factory next to a single resident, the choices of the entitlement and the remedy for protecting the entitlement have distributional consequences. Given the entitlement, a party is generally better off if it is protected by an injunctive remedy rather than by a damage remedy (with liability equal to actual damages); although the damage remedy guarantees that the protected party will be fully compensated for damages, the injunctive remedy gives that party the right to hold out for more. Under either remedy, a party is also obviously better off if the entitlement is more favorable to that party.

In the pollution control example in Chapter 12, in which the pollution victims are third parties, the distributional effects of the choice between strict liability and negligence to control the polluting industry are similar to those discussed in the automobile accident context. Under negligence, the victims bear their own losses, whereas under strict liability the producers — and ultimately consumers of the product — bear these losses. In general then, whenever the parties to a dispute are "strangers" — that is, not in a contractual or market relationship — the choice of legal rules will have distributional consequences.

Should Legal Rules Be Used to Redistribute Income?

Having now identified the types of situations in which the legal system is most likely to have distributional effects, we can return to the question of whether legal rules *should* be used in these situations to promote distributional equity. The answer to this question depends in part on the "cost" of using legal rules to redistribute income relative to the cost of using taxes or transfers. Legal redistribution may be costly in the sense that inefficient rules may have to be chosen in order to achieve the desired result. For example, recall the discussion in Chapter 9 of driver-pedestrian accidents in which both parties are risk averse and the pedestrian cannot affect expected losses. It was seen that negligence is efficient because the driver will meet the standard of care and the pedestrian will be able to buy a first-party accident insurance policy with full coverage; strict liability may not be efficient because of the moral hazard problem (which could result in the driver not being able to buy a liability insurance policy with full coverage and/or in the driver not taking appropriate care). But if drivers are wealthier than pedestrians, strict liability may be preferable to negligence on equity grounds. The loss of efficiency from using strict liability rather than negligence is a "cost" of redistributing income from drivers as a class to pedestrians as a class.

There may be instances in which redistribution through the legal system is not costly in this sense. For example, suppose that in some types of nuisance disputes the parties can be counted on to bargain in a cooperative way. Then, for the reasons discussed in Chapter 4, any entitlement will lead to the efficient outcome, whether protected by an injunctive remedy or a damage remedy. Thus, the choice of the entitlement and the remedy can be used to redistribute income without causing an inefficient resolution of the nuisance dispute. In general, however, not all legal rules will be efficient, so it often will be necessary to choose an inefficient legal rule in order to promote equity.

An additional consideration in deciding whether to use the legal system to promote distributional equity is the "precision" of legal redistribution. Legal rules will not be able to redistribute income systematically unless the status of the parties in a certain type of dispute corresponds closely to the groups between which redistribution is desired. For example, in automobile accidents involving drivers and pedestrians, there probably is not a close correspondence between the income of a party and whether that party is a driver or a pedestrian. Perhaps higher income persons are more likely to be drivers than pedestrians, but there are certainly many low-income drivers and high-income pedestrians. Thus, liability rules regarding driver-pedestrian accidents are not very precise instruments for accomplishing income redistribution. In nuisance and pollution control disputes, there may be a closer correspondence between the income of a party and whether that party is a victim or an injurer. For example, the consumers of the output of some polluting industry may be mainly higher income people, while the victims living near the polluting factories may be primarily lower income persons. Thus, in some kinds of disputes, the choice of a legal rule might contribute towards the implementation of distributional goals.

However, even when there is a close correspondence between the status of the parties in a certain kind of dispute and the groups between which redistribution is desired, legal rules still might not be able to achieve redistribution as systematically as an income tax system. The reason is simply that redistribution through the legal system may only occur when a dispute arises, and not all members of a given income class will be involved in a dispute. For example, even if the output of a polluting industry were consumed exclusively by rich persons and the pollution victims were all poor persons, not every rich person necessarily purchases this commodity and not every poor person lives near a factory in this industry. Thus, the legal rule used to control the pollution dispute will, at best, redistribute income from a subset of one income class to a subset of another.[70] In general then, the legal system is not as precise as the tax system in redistributing income by income classes.

The initial discussion of efficiency and equity in Chapter 2 showed that, if it is costly to redistribute income, there may be a

70. The point of this example may not be fully applicable in some legal contexts. For example, consider driver-pedestrian accidents and suppose that drivers would purchase liability insurance if strict liability is chosen and pedestrians would purchase first-party accident insurance if negligence is chosen. Then, even though only a fraction of all drivers and only a fraction of all pedestrians may be involved in an accident, the choice between strict liability and negligence will affect everyone because of insurance. The point of the pollution example in the text would then apply only to the extent that the insurance coverage is incomplete.

tradeoff between efficiency and equity. In other words, it may be desirable to choose an inefficient policy in order to promote the desired distribution of income. The present chapter has shown that income redistribution *is* generally costly, whether it is accomplished by the tax and transfer system or by the legal system. Nonetheless, several reasons have been suggested in this chapter why the choice of legal rules should be based primarily on efficiency considerations. In some circumstances — contractual disputes — legal rules often will have little or no effect on the distribution of income. In situations in which the legal system does have distributional consequences — disputes between strangers — legal rules still should be based primarily on efficiency considerations because legal rules are generally less precise than taxes and transfers as a means of redistributing income and may be more costly. Thus, the justification for the assumption made at the end of Chapter 2 — that income could be costlessly redistributed — is not only that this simplified the subsequent exposition by allowing us to focus on the efficiency analysis of legal rules. As this chapter has shown, the justification is also that, even when the cost of redistributing income is taken into account, there are reasons why the efficiency analysis should be of principal importance.

CHAPTER 15

A SUMMING UP

Now that we have completed the discussion of the relationship between efficiency and equity and have examined several applications of the efficiency criterion to legal problems, the major themes of the book can be summarized. These themes will be presented in the form of three questions that should be considered in every economic analysis of a legal problem. The first question is concerned with choosing the criterion for evaluating legal rules. The second and third questions are concerned with determining the effectiveness of legal rules in satisfying the criterion. As these questions are discussed below, the reader should refer to Figure 1, which shows the relationships among them.

The Efficiency-Equity Question

Should efficiency be the sole criterion used to evaluate legal rules, or should equity be taken into account as well? Since this question has just been answered at length in the previous chapter, not much needs to be said here. In disputes in which the parties are in a contractual or market relationship — as in the breach of contract and products liability examples — efficiency usually should be the only criterion because it is very difficult, if not impossible, to redistribute income. In disputes in which the parties are, in actuality or in effect, strangers — as in the nuisance law, automobile accident, and pollution control examples — it is possible to promote the equitable distribution of income through the legal system, but this usually can be done better through the government's tax and transfer system. Thus,

FIGURE 1
A SUMMING UP

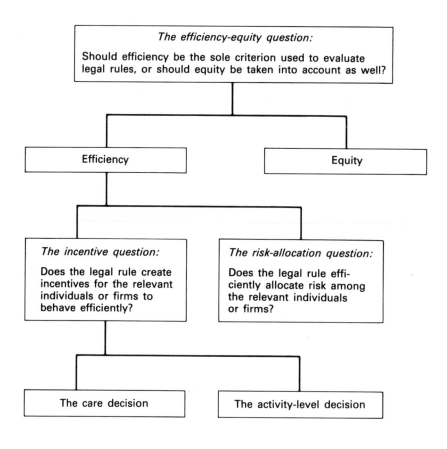

efficiency generally should be the primary criterion for evaluating legal rules. Given this criterion, there are two key aspects of efficiency that determine the extent to which legal rules satisfy the criterion: incentives and risk allocation.

The Incentive Question

Does the legal rule create incentives for the relevant individuals or firms to behave efficiently? "Efficient behavior" here means behavior that maximizes aggregate benefits less aggregate costs. Since individuals and firms naturally consider the effects of their behavior on their own benefits and costs, the incentive problem for legal rules is how to induce individuals and firms to take into account the effects of their behavior on the benefits and costs of others. There are two aspects of behavior that are encompassed within the incentive question: the *care decision* and the *activity-level decision.*

The *care decision* refers generally to the behavior of an individual or a firm that affects costs and benefits, *taking as given* the individual's or the firm's level of participation in the activity that is the source of the dispute. (What is meant by "level of participation in the activity" will become clear in the next paragraph.) The term *care* applies most naturally to the automobile accident and products liability examples, in which care corresponds, for example, to how fast the driver drives, to whether the pedestrian walks or runs, and to whether the soda manufacturer uses bottles or cans. It also applies readily to the pollution control example, in which care corresponds to whether the polluter filters or not.

The term *care* is meant, however, to apply more generally. In the nuisance law example, because the output of the factory is assumed to determine the amount of pollution, care can refer either to the factory's output or to the amount of pollution. In the breach of contract example, care corresponds both to the seller's decision whether to breach when a third-party offer is made and to the buyer's investment in reliance. And in the law enforcement example, care corresponds to the residents' decisions whether to double-park. Thus, in every application we examined, the legal system was evaluated in terms of whether it created incentives for the relevant individuals or firms to take the appropriate amount of care.

The *activity-level decision* refers generally either to the number of individuals or firms who choose to participate in the activity that is the source of the dispute, or to the extent of each individual's or firm's participation in such an activity. Of the applications we have discussed, this decision arose explicitly only in the automobile accident, pollution control, and products liability examples. In the automobile accident example, the driver's activity level corresponded to how much he drove and the pedestrian's activity level was represented by how frequently he traveled by foot rather than by some alternative mode of transportation. Each party's decision about how much to participate in the activity affected his own benefits and the expected accident costs. In the pollution control and products liability examples, the activity level corresponded to the level of output of the industry. This was determined by consumers' decisions about how much of the good to purchase, which affected their own benefits and, respectively, pollution damages or expected accident costs. Thus, in the automobile accident, pollution control, and products liability examples, legal rules were evaluated both in terms of whether they created incentives for the parties to take the appropriate amount of care and in terms of whether they created incentives for the parties to engage in the activity at an appropriate level. Although the activity-level issue was not discussed in the other applications, it could have been in some of them.[71]

In general, therefore, the incentive aspect of efficiency will encompass both a care decision and an activity-level decision, and legal rules should be evaluated with respect to their effects on both decisions. We can now turn to the second key aspect of efficiency.

71. Consider, for example, the nuisance law application, which was based on an example of a polluting factory next to a single resident. As noted in the previous paragraph, because the factory's output was assumed to determine the amount of pollution, output or pollution can be treated interchangeably as representing the factory's care. If we had considered the effects of nuisance remedies on the *number* of factories locating near the pollution victim, there would also have been an activity-level issue.

The Risk-Allocation Question

Does the legal rule efficiently allocate risk among the relevant individuals or firms? We saw in the discussion of risk bearing and insurance in Chapter 7 that it is desirable to reduce the risk borne by a risk-averse party. This is true whether the risk is a beneficial one (when the uncertainty is about how much one will gain) or a detrimental one (when the uncertainty is about how much one will lose). If the risk cannot be (or is not) eliminated, then it should be allocated among the relevant individuals or firms according to their relative aversion to risk. This may mean that the risk should be shared among the parties, or shifted entirely to one of them, or, if relevant, shifted to an insurance company.

The risk-allocation issue was discussed in the context of the breach of contract, automobile accident, products liability, and law enforcement examples. In the first example, we saw how the remedies for breach of contract allocate the beneficial risk of a higher third-party offer between the seller and the buyer. In the automobile accident and products liability examples, we saw how liability rules allocate the detrimental risk of an accident between the injurer (a driver or a manufacturer, depending on the example) and the victim (a pedestrian or a consumer). And in the law enforcement example, we saw how the risk-bearing costs of an enforcement system are determined by the choice of how much to invest in detecting violators and how much to fine them. In each example, the legal system was evaluated in terms of how well it promoted the optimal allocation or bearing of risk.

The goal of reducing risk-bearing costs by compensating victims of accidents is sometimes confused with the goal of promoting distributional equity. The source of this confusion is easiest to see in the context of the automobile accident example. Suppose the driver is risk neutral and the pedestrian is risk averse but cannot obtain first-party accident insurance. There is then an efficiency argument for using the rule of strict liability to compensate the pedestrian for his losses. This argument is based on risk-allocation considerations, not equity considerations. However, using the rule of strict liability rather than the rule of negligence also has distributional consequences. In effect, it redistributes the expected accident losses from the class of pedestrians to the class of drivers. Whether this is desirable on equity grounds is a separate matter. In general, there is an efficiency basis for using the legal system to reduce the bearing of risk. The resulting distributional effects should be evaluated separately.

In thinking about both the risk-allocation question and the incentive question, it is also important to consider the relationship between private insurance and legal rules. As seen in the context of the automobile accident and products liability examples, if an ideal insurance policy is available — meaning a policy with full coverage and a premium that reflects the insured party's expected losses — then the legal system does not need to take risk-allocation concerns into account. However, if the policy does not provide complete coverage, then it may be desirable to base legal rules in part on risk-allocation considerations. Also, if the premium does not reflect expected losses, the policy may adversely affect the incentives of the insured party. This is the moral hazard problem first discussed in Chapter 7. Thus, in general, the optimal choice of legal rules and policies to deal with incentive and risk-allocation issues depends in part on the availability and nature of private insurance.

This summary of the themes of the book highlights a point that has already been seen in some of the specific applications: The legal system generally cannot accomplish every objective. Tradeoffs may have to be made between promoting efficiency and promoting equity. Even if efficiency is the only goal, there may be a conflict between incentive issues and risk-allocation issues. And even if only incentive considerations are relevant, a legal rule may not be able to simultaneously induce efficient care decisions and efficient activity-level decisions. However, as we have seen in specific applications, the inability of the legal system to achieve every objective does not mean that the economic approach to law is necessarily indeterminate and unhelpful. On the contrary, the fact that there are many goals that the legal system might be viewed as trying to accomplish makes economic analysis all the more helpful in determining what the tradeoffs are among the goals and how to strike an appropriate balance.

CHAPTER 16
CONCLUSION

As noted in the introduction, the goal of this book has been to convey a sense of how to "think like an economist" about legal rules and policies. Thus, many simplifying assumptions have been made and the legal system has intentionally been described in a somewhat abstract way. In this concluding chapter, some of the practical difficulties in employing economic analysis to study law will be discussed.

The Problem of Valuation

Probably the most difficult problem in undertaking an economic analysis of a legal rule or policy is putting dollar values on the relevant costs and benefits. The dollar values should be determined by the affected individuals (provided one accepts the principle of consumer sovereignty discussed briefly at the end of Chapter 2). It is easy to infer the value an individual would place on a cost or benefit if the loss or gain involves a standardized good that is sold in a market. The value is simply the price of the good. For example, suppose that in a breach of contract dispute a buyer's loss consists solely of having to repurchase in the marketplace a good that was supposed to have been delivered by some particular seller. This loss is easily valued by the price of this good at the time of breach (plus any incidental costs associated with the transaction). However, the valuation process is much more difficult if the loss or gain involves a nonstandardized or unique good. For example, suppose as a result of pollution someone is forced to move from his home. Although the market price of the home could be determined from the sales prices of similar homes, this price will not reflect the special attachment the person who lived there may have had for that location and house.

In situations in which the losses or gains involve nonmarketed or nonstandardized items, one could in principle ask the affected individual how much he values the loss or gain. However, this approach is hindered by the obvious problem that losers may have an incentive to overstate their losses — they would, for example, if their compensation is based on their stated losses. Similarly, gainers may have an incentive to understate their gains.

Moreover, even if it were possible to overcome these problems, there would be the following ambiguity. With respect to a loss, should the question be "How much would you be willing to pay to avoid the loss?" or "How much would you have to be paid to allow the loss to be imposed upon you?" The answers to these questions are not generally the same. For example, suppose you are a very noise-sensitive person involved in a dispute with your neighbor over the loudness of his stereo and suppose you have little wealth — say $5,000. You might be willing to pay a large fraction of your wealth — say $3,000 — for quiet, but you might not accept less than $10,000 to allow his noise to be imposed upon you. In deciding whether to assign an entitlement to noise or quiet (or some intermediate entitlement), should a court treat the value of quiet as $3,000 or $10,000? The same kind of ambiguity also would arise in valuing gains.

These ambiguities are due to what economists call *wealth effects*. Wealth effects occur in situations in which a person places a high value, relative to his wealth, on the loss or gain in question. To see what is meant by a wealth effect, note that the question "How much would you be willing to pay to avoid the loss?" implicitly assumes that you will suffer the loss unless you pay to avoid it, whereas the question "How much would you have to be paid to allow the loss to be imposed upon you?" implicitly assumes that you will not suffer the loss. If you value the loss highly, then you are, in effect, much poorer when you are asked the first question than when you are asked the second. It is not surprising, then, that the answer to the first question is less than the answer to the second. This is why the ambiguity is said to be due to a wealth effect. If the loss in question is not an "important" one in this sense, then the answers to the two questions will be very close to each other and the ambiguity will, for all practical purposes, disappear. In general, however, these two questions will produce different answers.

Because of the above difficulties, the practical implementation of economic analysis usually will require a somewhat arbitrary method to determine the value of losses and gains involving nonmarketed or nonstandardized items. There are many procedures that have been developed by economists to estimate these values. For example, it may be possible to infer the value placed on quiet by examining how much more homes in quiet neighborhoods sell for, everything else equal (everything else can be held equal by statistical methods). The values derived from this procedure obviously reflect a representative or average person's values. Thus, the value of quiet for an especially noise-sensitive person will be understated, and vice versa. In practice, any procedure used to estimate dollar values for costs or benefits will make some mistakes of this kind.

The problem of assigning dollar values to costs and benefits is particularly difficult when life or limb is involved. An individual presumably would give up all of his wealth to avoid the certainty of being killed and would not accept any amount of money to voluntarily be killed. The same is probably true with respect to loss of limbs. Thus, it may seem that economic analysis cannot deal with situations in which life or limb is involved. If this were true, it would especially constrain the economic analysis of law since many legal disputes involve loss of life or limb.

However, the fact that individuals would not voluntarily sacrifice life or limb for any amount of money is not directly relevant to situations in which life or limb is at risk. The relevant question then is "How much would you be willing to pay to reduce the *probability* of bodily harm?" or "How much would you have to be paid to accept an increase in the probability of bodily harm?" These are questions that individuals implicitly answer every day. For example, individuals frequently are willing to pay more to fly rather than to drive, not only because it is faster, but also because it is safer. Similarly, many laborers are willing to work in riskier industries in part because of the higher wages they can obtain. Although any procedure used to estimate the value of changing the probability of loss of life or limb will be somewhat arbitrary because of the problems discussed above, there is no fundamental reason why economic analysis cannot be applied to these kinds of situations.

Despite what has been said, there undoubtedly will be instances in which it will be very difficult or impossible to arrive at reasonable values for certain costs or benefits. While this problem arises with the use of economic analysis generally, it may be especially relevant to the economic analysis of law because legal disputes often involve losses or gains that are difficult to value. Some critics of economic analysis have suggested that the problem of valuation may lead to a bias in the economic approach, in that the categories of costs or benefits that are hard to quantify will tend to be ignored. Other critics have suggested that because of the difficulty of quantifying certain costs or benefits, the economic analyst will tend to substitute his own subjective values for these items, and therefore the analysis may simply "confirm" his prior beliefs. Both of these arguments may have merit in some instances. But they should be seen as potential criticisms of economic *analysts* rather than of economic *analysis.* The analyst should be careful to consider all relevant costs and benefits, including those hard to value. He also should be careful to state his assumptions and methods explicitly so that others can decide whether prior beliefs or careful analysis have determined the conclusion. Despite these potential problems, economic analysis has been found to be very helpful in the design of public policy in many areas. There is no fundamental reason why it should not be just as useful in the examination of the legal system.

BIBLIOGRAPHICAL APPENDIX

The primary purpose of the appendix is to provide a guide to the law and economics literature upon which this book is based. A few articles that develop ideas closely related to those contained in the book also will be mentioned. (Readers interested in examining additional material should consult the sources cited at the end of the appendix.)

The points made in the chapter on the Coase Theorem derive from Ronald H. Coase's classic article, The Problem of Social Cost, 3 J.L. & Econ. 1 (1960). During the past two decades, dozens of articles have been written about the Coase Theorem. The ones that are most relevant to this book are concerned with the effects of strategic behavior on the bargaining process. See, for example, Donald H. Regan, The Problem of Social Cost Revisited, 15 J.L. & Econ. 427, 427-432 (1972), and Robert Cooter, The Cost of Coase, 11 J. Legal Stud. 1, 14-29 (1982).

The chapter on nuisance law draws heavily on my own work, especially A. Mitchell Polinsky, Resolving Nuisance Disputes: The Simple Economics of Injunctive and Damage Remedies, 32 Stan. L. Rev. 1075 (1980).[72] That paper builds upon the foundation laid by Guido Calabresi and A. Douglas Melamed in their path-breaking article, Property Rules, Liability Rules and Inalienability: One View of the Cathedral, 85 Harv. L. Rev. 1089 (1972). For other closely related discussions of these issues, see, for example, Frank I. Michelman, Pollution as a Tort: A Non-Accidental Perspective on Calabresi's Costs, 80 Yale L.J. 647, 669-673 (1971), Robert C. Ellickson, Alternatives to Zoning:

72. Copyright © 1980 by the Board of Trustees of the Leland Stanford Junior University. Excerpts reprinted by permission.

Covenants, Nuisance Rules, and Fines as Land Use Controls, 40 U. Chi. L. Rev. 681, 738-748 (1973), and Richard A. Posner, Economic Analysis of Law 44-52 (2d ed. 1977).

The results described in the first chapter on breach of contract remedies — in which the parties are assumed to be neutral with respect to risk — are developed formally in an important article by Steven Shavell, Damage Measures for Breach of Contract, 11 Bell J. Econ. 466 (1980). For extensions of this analysis, see William P. Rogerson, Efficient Reliance and Contract Remedies, Social Science Working Paper 340, Division of the Humanities and Social Sciences, California Institute of Technology (August 1980), and Steven Shavell, On the Design of Contracts and Remedies for Breach, Q.J. Econ. (forthcoming). The second chapter on breach of contract remedies — which focuses on risk-allocation issues — follows closely the discussion in an article of my own, A. Mitchell Polinsky, Risk Sharing Through Breach of Contract Remedies, 12 J. Legal Stud. — (1983).[73] For some closely related analyses, see Lewis A. Kornhauser, Breach of Contract in the Presence of Risk Aversion, Reliance, and Reputation, IP-284, Working Papers in Economic Theory and Econometrics, Center for Research in Management Science, Institute of Business and Economic Research, University of California, Berkeley (February 1980), at 12-19, and Steven Shavell, On the Design of Contracts and Remedies for Breach, Q.J. Econ. 8-9, 27-28 (forthcoming) (page citations are to Working Paper No. 727, National Bureau of Economic Research (August 1981)). Other relevant discussions of breach of contract include those by John H. Barton, The Economic Basis of Damages for Breach of Contract, 1 J. Legal Stud. 277 (1972), Charles J. Goetz & Robert E. Scott, Liquidated Damages, Penalties and the Just Compensation Principle: Some Notes on an Enforcement Model and a Theory of Efficient Breach, 77 Colum. L. Rev. 554 (1977), and Richard A. Posner, Economic Analysis of Law 74-79, 88-94 (2d ed. 1977).

The first chapter on automobile accidents was concerned both with the care exercised by the parties and with the extent of

73. Copyright © 1983 by The University of Chicago. Excerpts reprinted by permission of The University of Chicago Press.

their participation in the relevant activity. The discussion of the care issue derives generally from the pioneering article by John Prather Brown, Toward an Economic Theory of Liability, 2 J. Legal Stud. 323 (1973), while the discussion of the activity-level issue is based on Steven Shavell, Strict Liability Versus Negligence, 9 J. Legal Stud. 1 (1980). See also Peter A. Diamond, Single Activity Accidents, 3 J. Legal Stud. 104 (1974). The second chapter on automobile accidents — which focuses on risk-allocation and insurance issues — derives generally from Steven Shavell, On Liability and Insurance, 13 Bell J. Econ. 120 (1982). For some other discussions of accident law of related interest, see, for example, Guido Calabresi, The Costs of Accidents: A Legal and Economic Analysis (1970), Guido Calabresi, Optimal Deterrence and Accidents, 84 Yale L.J. 656 (1975), and Richard A. Posner, Economic Analysis of Law 119-161 (2d ed. 1977).

The first part of the chapter on law enforcement — in which the individuals whose behavior is being controlled are assumed to be risk neutral — develops ideas first formalized in a classic paper by Gary S. Becker, Crime and Punishment: An Economic Approach, 76 J. Pol. Econ. 169 (1968). Some closely related discussions include those by George J. Stigler, The Optimum Enforcement of Laws, 78 J. Pol. Econ. 526 (1970), Richard A. Posner, Economic Analysis of Law 164-172 (2d ed. 1977), and Steven Shavell and myself, A. Mitchell Polinsky & Steven Shavell, The Optimal Use of Fines and Imprisonment, Working Paper No. 6, Law and Economics Program, Stanford Law School (September 1982). The second part of the chapter — in which the individuals are assumed to be risk averse — is based generally on another paper I wrote with Steven Shavell, A. Mitchell Polinsky & Steven Shavell, The Optimal Tradeoff Between the Probability and Magnitude of Fines, 69 Am. Econ. Rev. 880 (1979). For an application of some of the ideas in this chapter to antitrust enforcement, see Kenneth G. Elzinga & William Breit, The Antitrust Penalties: A Study in Law and Economics 112-138 (1976), and Michael K. Block & Joseph Gregory Sidak, The Cost of Antitrust Deterrence: Why Not Hang a Price Fixer Now and Then?, 68 Geo. L.J. 1131 (1980).

The basic idea developed in the chapter on pollution control is implicit in an article by Guido Calabresi, Some Thoughts on

Risk Distribution and the Law of Torts, 70 Yale L.J. 499, 500-507 (1961), and is stated more explicitly by Richard B. Stewart & James E. Krier, Environmental Law and Policy: Readings, Materials and Notes 227 (2d ed. 1978). It is formalized in a paper of my own, A. Mitchell Polinsky, Strict Liability vs. Negligence in a Market Setting, 70 Am. Econ. Rev.: Papers & Proc. 363 (1980). An essentially identical discussion is contained in an article by Steven Shavell, Strict Liability Versus Negligence, 9 J. Legal Stud. 1, 3, 14 (1980).

The analysis of strict liability in the chapter on products liability derives generally from an important article by A. Michael Spence, Consumer Misperceptions, Product Failure and Producer Liability, 44 Rev. Econ. Stud. 561 (1977). Spence's analysis was expanded to include negligence in a paper by Steven Shavell, Strict Liability Versus Negligence, 9 J. Legal Stud. 1, 3-5, 14-16 (1980). Other closely related discussions include those by Dennis Epple & Artur Raviv, Product Safety: Liability Rules, Market Structure, and Imperfect Information, 68 Am. Econ. Rev. 80 (1978), and by William Rogerson and myself, A. Mitchell Polinsky & William P. Rogerson, Products Liability, Consumer Misperceptions, and Market Power, Working Paper No. 4, Law and Economics Program, Stanford Law School (July 1982).

Since the purely economic topics dealt with in the book — efficiency and equity, risk bearing and insurance, and competitive markets — are all standard fare for students of economics, the discussions of these topics are not based on particular articles. However, noneconomist readers interested in further general reading on these topics might consult two articles by Kenneth J. Arrow, one by Bruce A. Ackerman, and one of my own. See Kenneth J. Arrow, The Organization of Economic Activity: Issues Pertinent to the Choice of Market Versus Nonmarket Allocation, in Public Expenditures and Policy Analysis 59-73 (Robert H. Haveman & Julius Margolis eds. 1970), Kenneth J. Arrow, Essays in the Theory of Risk-Bearing 134-143 (1971), Bruce A. Ackerman, Introduction: On the Role of Economic Analysis in Property Law, in Economic Foundations of Property Law vii-xvi (Bruce A. Ackerman ed. 1975), and A. Mitchell Polinsky, Economic Analysis as a Potentially Defective Product: A Buyer's Guide to Posner's *Economic Analysis of Law,* 87 Harv. L. Rev. 1655 (1974).

The more specific issue of whether legal rules can and should be used to redistribute income has been discussed by several authors. For example, the general point that legal rules can more easily redistribute income in noncontractual situations than in contractual ones is made by Harold Demsetz, Wealth Distribution and the Ownership of Rights, 1 J. Legal Stud. 223 (1972). A similar point is made with respect to products liability rules by Koichi Hamada, Liability Rules and Income Distribution in Product Liability, 66 Am. Econ. Rev. 228 (1976). Whether legal rules should be used to redistribute income has been discussed in general terms in articles by, among others, Steven Shavell and by me. See Steven Shavell, A Note on Efficiency vs. Distributional Equity in Legal Rulemaking: Should Distributional Equity Matter Given Optimal Income Taxation?, 71 Am. Econ. Rev.: Papers & Proc. 414 (1981), and A. Mitchell Polinsky, Economic Analysis as a Potentially Defective Product: A Buyer's Guide to Posner's *Economic Analysis of Law*, 87 Harv. L. Rev. 1655 (1974).[74] The redistributive function of legal rules has also been discussed in specific legal contexts by, for example, Bruce A. Ackerman, Regulating Slum Housing Markets On Behalf of the Poor: Of Housing Codes, Housing Subsidies and Income Redistribution Policy, 80 Yale L.J. 1093 (1971), Anthony T. Kronman, Contract Law and Distributive Justice, 89 Yale L. J. 472 (1980), Guido Calabresi & A. Douglas Melamed, Property Rules, Liability Rules and Inalienability: One View of the Cathedral, 85 Harv. L. Rev. 1089 (1972), and by me, A. Mitchell Polinsky, Resolving Nuisance Disputes: The Simple Economics of Injunctive and Damage Remedies, 32 Stan. L. Rev. 1075 (1980). See also Richard A. Epstein, The Social Consequences of Common Law Rules, 95 Harv. L. Rev. 1717 (1982).

One of the issues discussed in the concluding chapter of the book was the difficulty of valuing gains and losses when there are wealth effects. This issue was first highlighted in a legal context by Ezra J. Mishan, Pareto Optimality and the Law, 19

74. My current views about the appropriateness of using the legal system to redistribute income — which are explained in Chapters 2 and 14 of this book — differ somewhat from the views reflected in this and other earlier articles. In brief, I now see a more limited role for distributional considerations in the choice of legal rules and policies.

Oxford Econ. Papers 255 (1967). It continues to receive attention. See, for example, Duncan Kennedy, Cost-Benefit Analysis of Entitlement Problems, 33 Stan. L. Rev. 387 (1981). Another issue discussed in the concluding chapter was the difficulty of valuing life and limb. Many approaches to this problem have been developed by economists. For a survey of some of them, see, for example, Michael W. Jones-Lee, The Value of Life: An Economic Analysis (1976). The concluding chapter also referred to critics of economic analysis who argue either that categories of costs or benefits that are difficult to quantify will tend to be ignored, or that the economic analyst will tend to substitute his own subjective values for these costs or benefits. For some discussions of this sort, see, for example, Laurence H. Tribe, Policy Science: Analysis or Ideology?, 2 Phil. & Pub. Aff. 66 (1972), Frank I. Michelman, Norms and Normativity in the Economic Theory of Law, 62 Minn. L. Rev. 1015 (1978), and Mario J. Rizzo, The Mirage of Efficiency, 8 Hofstra L. Rev. 641 (1980).

Readers interested in examining additional material can find it in a variety of sources. There are several books on law and economics, the most influential of which have been Guido Calabresi's The Costs of Accidents: A Legal and Economic Analysis (1970), and Richard A. Posner's Economic Analysis of Law (2d ed. 1977). Other books of interest include R. W. Anderson, The Economics of Crime (1976), Kenneth G. Elzinga & William Breit, The Antitrust Penalties: A Study in Law and Economics (1976), Werner Z. Hirsch, Law and Economics: An Introductory Analysis (1979), William A. Luksetich & Michael D. White, Crime and Public Policy: An Economic Approach (1982), J. M. Oliver, Law and Economics: An Introduction (1979), Llad Phillips & Harold L. Votey, Jr., The Economics of Crime Control (1981), Richard A. Posner, Antitrust Law: An Economic Perspective (1976), Richard A. Posner, The Economics of Justice (1981), and Gordon Tullock, The Logic of the Law (1971). For a useful introduction to several of these books, see Robert Cooter, Law and the Imperialism of Economics: An Introduction to the Economic Analysis of Law and a Review of the Major Books, 29 U.C.L.A. L. Rev. 1260 (1982).

There are also many collections of articles on law and economics, appearing either as books or as law review symposia. Some of the more recently published books are Essays on the Economics of Crime and Punishment (Gary S. Becker & William M. Landes eds. 1974), Economic Foundations of Property Law (Bruce A. Ackerman ed. 1975), The Economics of Legal Relationships: Readings in the Theory of Property Rights (Henry G. Manne ed. 1975), Perspectives on Tort Law (Robert L. Rabin ed. 1976), The Economics of Medical Malpractice (Simon Rottenberg ed. 1978), Economic Analysis and Antitrust Law (Terry Calvani & John Siegfried eds. 1979), The Economics of Contract Law (Anthony T. Kronman & Richard A. Posner eds. 1979), Economics of Corporation Law and Securities Regulation (Richard A. Posner & Kenneth E. Scott eds. 1980), The Economics of Crime (Ralph Andreano & John J. Siegfried eds. 1980), and The Economic Approach to Law (Paul Burrows & Cento G. Veljanovski eds. 1981). The recently published law review symposia include Private Alternatives to the Judicial Process, 8 J. Legal Stud. 231 (1979), Symposium on Efficiency as a Legal Concern, 8 Hofstra L. Rev. 485 (1980), A Response to the Efficiency Symposium, 8 Hofstra L. Rev. 811 (1980), Change in the Common Law: Legal and Economic Perspectives, 9 J. Legal Stud. 189 (1980), and The Law and Economics of Privacy, 9 J. Legal Stud. 621 (1980).

A few law school casebooks also use economic analysis extensively. These include Richard A. Posner, Tort Law: Cases and Economic Analysis (1982), Richard A. Posner & Frank H. Easterbrook, Antitrust Cases, Economic Notes, and Other Materials (2d ed. 1981), and Richard B. Stewart & James E. Krier, Environmental Law and Policy: Readings, Materials and Notes (2d ed. 1978).

Postscript: I have been unable to find a source for the story of the beans and the can opener used in the introductory chapter of the book. As far as I know, it exists solely as part of the "oral" tradition of the economics profession.

INDEX

105-107
conflict between efficiency and
equity, 7-10, 105, 112-113, 120
costless, 9-10
costly, 8-10, 105-107, 110-111
Income taxes. *See* Taxes
Incompletely specified contract. *See*
Contracts, incompletely
specified
Inefficient violations of laws. *See*
Crimes
Information, imperfect
automobile accident remedies,
39, 40, 46-47
breach of contract remedies, 35-36
consumer misperception of
product risks, 97-99
insurance, 54-55, 69-70
mistakes in law enforcement, 83
nuisance law remedies, 20-23
Injunction, in nuisance law, 15, 17,
18-19, 21, 22, 23, 110
Insurance, 52, 53-55, 68-71, 100-101,
120
Insurance premium. *See* Insurance
Intermediate entitlement. *See*
Entitlement, in nuisance law

Law enforcement, 73-84
Level of participation in an activity.
See Activity level
Liability. *See* Damages, in nuisance
law; Expectation damages, for
breach of contract; Liquidated
damages, for breach of contract;
Negligence; Reliance damages,
for breach of contract;
Restitution damages, for breach
of contract; Strict liability
Liability insurance. *See* Insurance
Life, valuation of, 10, 125-126. *See
also* Nonstandardized goods,
valuation of
Limb, valuation of, 10, 125-126. *See
also* Nonstandardized goods,
valuation of
Liquidated damages, for breach of
contract, 61-63
Long-run equilibrium, in
competitive markets, 85-87

Measurement of costs and benefits.
See Valuation of costs and
benefits
Minimizing transaction costs. *See*
Coase Theorem; Transaction
costs
Mistakes, in law enforcement, 83
Moral hazard. *See* Insurance

Negligence
automobile accidents, 39-40,
43-44, 46-48, 67, 69, 70-71,
109-111, 119-120
pollution control, 90-91, 92, 110
products liability, 97, 98, 99-101,
102, 103-104, 109
No liability, and products liability,
97, 98-99, 99
Noneconomic accident costs. *See*
Accident costs, noneconomic
Nonmarketed goods. *See*
Nonstandardized goods,
valuation of
Nonstandardized goods, valuation
of, 123-124. *See also* Accident
costs, noneconomic;
Standardized goods, valuation of
Nuisance law remedies
damages, 15-16, 17, 19-20, 21-23,
110
injunction, 15, 17, 18-19, 21, 22,
23, 110

Optimal deterrence, 75-76. *See also*
Crimes; Efficient violations of
laws
Optimal risk allocation
automobile accidents, 66-68
contractual relationships, 58-60
generally, 119-120
products liability, 99-101

Pollution control remedies
negligence, 90-91, 92, 110
strict liability, 91, 92-93,
110
Positive transaction costs. *See*
Transaction costs